Ben Learns to Get Smart

and

The Hidden Dangers of AI in Learning

by

Roy J. Andersen

The Moving Quill Publishing House

MQ

Copyright © Roy Andersen. 2013

The right of Roy Andersen to be identified as the author of this work has been asserted by him in accordance with the Copyright Designs and Patents Act 1988. All rights reserved. No part of this publication may be reproduced, stored in a retrieval system, or transmitted, in any form or by any means, electronic, mechanical, photocopying, recording, or otherwise, without the prior written permission of the copyright owner.

Disclaimer:
The author and the publisher will assume no liability nor responsibility to any person or entity with respect to any loss or damage related directly or indirectly to the information in this book. Neither the author nor the publisher will provide any remedy for indirect, consequential, punitive, or incidental damages arising from this book, including such from negligence, strict liability, or breach of warranty or contract, even after notice of the possibility of such damages. Neither the publisher nor the author accept any responsibility for the actions of another based on the information in this book.

ISBN: 978-1-0683179-2-7

I would like to dedicate this book to

All the Children in the World.

May they grow up in happiness and live in a safer world than we now know.

Table of Contents

About Me	xi
What the Experts say	xv
Introduction	3
Ben's Story	19
Reflections:	49
Another Perspective of School	67
Eric	84
The Books of Roy Andersen	95
Reimagining Education for the AI Era	96
Whisperings of Betrayal	98
Intelligence: The Great Lie	99
Brain Plasticity	101
The Illusion of School	102
Is AI Making Our Kids Stupid?	103
The Real Dangers of AI	104
All that is Wrong with School:	
What teachers and parents can do to fix it.	106
Memoirs of a Happy Teacher /	
What Every Parent & Teacher Should Know	107
The Illusion of Education	108
For Parent For Teacher: Mediation	109
Teach Better Learn Better	110
Five Ways for Better Grades	111
Teaching and Learning in the 21st Century Online Course	118
References	122

Foreword

by

Dean Emeritus Gallaudet University, Washington D.C. U.S.A
Professor David Martin.

It is with pride and professional pleasure that I write this Foreword for a pioneering book authored by Roy Andersen. Today in the field of education, we are finally beginning once again (after a period of almost 50 years) to recognise the vital importance of cognitive development in our children.

This cognitive development is, for most individuals, a process that does not happen sufficiently in itself; it requires explicit activity on the part of parents, teachers, caregivers, and others. While we know that it's possible to acquire cognitive strategies in later life, it is never too late to improve one's thinking patterns, at the same time, early development by parents is essential whenever possible.

Even though most parents of young children today were not the beneficiaries themselves of systematic cognitive education in their own schooling, nonetheless it is not only possible but also necessary that they provide that foundation in thinking skills for their children, at an early age if possible.

Some will say that this development is the responsibility of the school, and of course, the school's role is of critical importance. However, we must remember that a school-age child may spend 40 hours or less per week in formal schooling (less in a number of countries), while there are 168 hours in the week (some of which, of course, should be spent in sleep). And formal schooling does not begin until after the development of some essential brain-patterning which can occur within the first two years of life.

This simple statistical comparison indicates that parents have the potential for at least as much, and perhaps more in some ways influence on their children's development as does the school. This important book designed as much for parents, as for teachers, indicates the rationale and process for how both can enhance the child's thinking process.

Clearly, the most powerful combination of forces would be the home and the school working together; helping schools to understand and implement the process of cognitive education for their part is the subject of other writings by Roy Andersen. With this book in hand, however, interested and dedicated parents can gain important understandings as well as procedures for their part in enabling tomorrow's adults to reach their fullest possible cognitive potential while there is still time to do so.

Prof. David Martin. PhD

Foreword Shared

by

Professor Luca Magni. LUISS Business School. Rome. Italy

It will probably take a few years, possibly even a decade before the public at large will get how revolutionary the ideas of Roy Andersen are.

His ideas resonate perfectly with the Learnable Theory and are destined to impact not only teaching in schools, but also the way human resources are selected and developed in organisations. Indeed, Roy's deconstruction of intelligence goes well beyond Daniel Coleman, Howard Gardner and what others have done so far. Roy goes at the root of learning, he links it to the creation and leveraging of meanings and how the symbolic process of language plays a key role in what we generally identify and name intelligence.

It is for these reasons that I am inclined to believe that Roy's ideas have the potential to promote a major turn around in multiple educational fields and practices, including Managerial Sciences.

Professor Luca Magni Ph.D

x

About Me

I did not do well in school. In fact, I failed every one of my final examinations and left school virtually illiterate. Yet, four years later, I was to pass all of these examinations and those considerably far, far higher with the highest distinction.

This achievement sparked in me a quest to understand not just what is wrong with the school system, but also how children learn and what hinders their learning. As I sought to improve the ways children could learn, I worked as a teacher through all the levels of education from kindergarten, through primary and secondary school and then in university.

For 45 years, I have struggled to share the thoughts and insights I gained with other teachers and parents on how children could learn better.

Eventually, I was to devise not only a new method of teaching but also a new understanding of what intelligence could be. It was inevitable from this background that I should become a consultant to help students of any age to better understand not just what they were learning, but how they could learn the skill of what we call intelligence.

As my experience in this developed, I was able to explain to my students the processes their mind and brain go through to understand their world, and the skills they can develop to explain their mind better to others to achieve far higher recognition. The classes I worked with improved in their overall performance, and the individuals I helped gained far higher grades.

I learned to understand that academic ability is not the same as intelligence. It is simply a matter of keeping up with numerous rules that build up a complexity of achievement. These rules are very simple and easy to understand, but only if each new rule is viewed from a competence with earlier rules.

The problem is that most students do not grasp a rule when it is being taught to them, because for many reasons, they are distracted, and by this struggle to understand what it means and how it may be applied. When this happens, which it does too frequently in a class of students, the student loses confidence in their ability to learn and soon becomes bored. To counter boredom, they invent distractions, which invariably affect the attention of those seeking to keep up with the lesson.

While one or two in the class have kept up with the rules and demonstrate great proficiency because of this, most struggle through different levels of confusion. Those who are the most confused are the poorest achievers and become known for their poor attitude in class. Unless, that is, something magical happens that causes them to want to learn to be better and become so. This, as you will now find, is what happens with the hero of our little story: Ben does learn to get smart.

This has important meanings to all children all over the world, but the presence of AI in education now raises concerns as to how it is lowering the intelligence of our children.

Therefore, in this book, we will learn how the human child gains their understanding of school and how, if they are so inspired, they can raise themselves from a poor performer to one of the very best. In sharp contrast to this, it will also show how AI is actually deteriorating the intelligence of our children, with the long-term implications behind this. As this book explores what is generally unknown at the moment, it hopes to inspire thoughts by which we may develop strategies to counter the effect of AI on the abilities of our children to learn to think.

It is vital that educationalists now and urgently move to devise means that will raise the intelligence of our youth by natural means, because they are the forbearers of a new species that is developing, and we must be neither apathetic nor lazy in this.

Roy Andersen

If you would like to know more of my work in education, the many books I have written or how to contact me for online lectures and conferences, please go to

www.andersenroy.com

What the Experts say:

"Roy's series of books clearly and methodically maps out exactly how students learn. He isn't afraid to address head-on the many misconceptions that are plaguing our society and thus having a negative impact on our students' learning. Parents and educators who read these books will not only have a better understanding, but will also be inspired to change in their attitudes and preconceived notions on how students can excel in their learning.

If you've ever wanted to unravel how students learn, then these books are the answer you have been looking for! They should be mandatory reading for every parent and educator."

Erin Calhoun. National Institute of Learning Development. USA

"What Every Parent and Teacher Should Know' (of which Ben Learns to Get Smart is a follow up) is written by a teacher who teaches from the heart. Every school should put this book in the hands of all school staff. School leaders should provide opportunities for weekly dialogue. These conversations can build teacher and student capacity toward teaching and learning."

Dr Gwendolyn Lavert. Educational Consultant. U.S.A.

"The most important books I have ever read about a child's intelligence."

Prof. Tatyana Oleinik. Pedagogical University. Ukraine.

"What Every Parent and Teacher Should Know appears to me to be very relevant to those currently teaching and particularly those who are just starting their career. Whilst presented as stories, they contextualize the learning process and provide clear and well-developed scenarios and ideas of problems faced by learners, reasons for them, and importantly, how teachers can start to address the different challenges they and their learners face in the mainstream classroom. In short, I think the book would make a great addition to any initial teacher training reading list."

Ian Arkell. Educational Consultant CEO SchoolPro. UK

"Roy's books should be read by every parent and educator in the world. They do represent a real breakthrough in our understanding of what intelligence is and how it develops, and the importance of changing the ways students are both parented and educated. Roy is doing for learning the work that is as significant as was that done in the past by such figures as John Dewey. These are must-reads for both parents and educators alike."

Dean Emeritus David Martin PhD Gallaudet University / Prof

USA .C.D ,Washington

"The whole set of Roy's books should be in the library of each school in every corner of the world. They should also be part of the syllabus in the institutions who are offering child psychology, and teacher training diplomas and degree programs, or at least they should be the part of a refresher course."

M.Imran Khan. CEO AIMMS Universities. Middle East

"These are very important and interesting books, with lots of valuable points for parents and teachers. They bring learning and education to a whole new level. Well done!"

Prof. Mads Hermansen. Educational Psychologist Denmark.

You can see more of the books I have written and more testimonials at

www.andersenroy.com

Ben Learns to Get Smart

and

The Hidden Dangers of AI in Learning

by

Roy J. Andersen

Introduction

The book is about a boy called Ben who is always in trouble, always late, always messing about, always getting low marks until, that is, something changes in him and he develops into the best in the class.

"The case of imaginary Ben highlights most of the troubles, misunderstandings, and confusions that exist in the minds and lives of too many children today. Andersen provides a masterful telling of how the mind of any student could learn to understand better, develop to be a more responsible member of the class, and significantly improve their class marks and exam grades in order to more successfully control the factors of their life after school.

This is another remarkable book by Roy J Andersen, as he continues to delight both parents and educators with his experiences and accounts of education and its need to evolve to better prepare our future generation as they move to face a world highly dominated by A.I."

Dean Emeritus/Professor David Martin Ph.D,
Gallaudet University, Washington, DC.

Ben Learns to Get Smart was never intended to be a big book. It is only an introduction to many other books, which more deeply explain how children really learn in school, and so far more of the real and very hidden dangers that AI is bringing into our civilization. Yet, in its few pages, you may glimpse all that is wrong with school and how any child may learn to improve their marks, grades, and so opportunities in life.

With the ready absorption of AI into education, many problems have suddenly come to light. We have the impression that AI will help us to think better, but recent studies have shown the very opposite. It is very important, therefore, that both parents and educationalists know of this, so that together they may devise means of improving the cognitive skills our youth are now beginning to lose through AI at a disturbing rate.

This is a very serious problem that will affect the intelligence of our species. In fact, a retired dean of an American university, a very dear and respected friend of mine, predicts that the forebrain will reduce in size through AI, causing us to think less. In an evolutionary sense, this is to say that our much later descendants will probably have a smaller skull.

Although, as I explain in *The Real Dangers of AI,* it seems inescapable that soon AI will be physically present within our body and within our brain, so that such descendants will be partially cyborg and more intelligent than we could ever naturally be. This would, however, mean that we would forever be a part of AI and no longer free to think as we individually are now.

Setting this aside, we are now faced with the present problems that AI is bringing into the school learning process. In fact, schools are struggling with how to cope with this level of technology in the education of children, for it is no simple thing. To date, the school has primarily focused on teaching computer skills, but AI has now largely taken over this fundamental skill. Now, students ask AI a question on their phone. They believe and trust the response they gain, and use this where they can to influence their teachers that they are worth a better mark.

The pressure on students to be the fastest and the brightest has always been a factor of school, as its prime purpose is to weed out those not capable of a university education. All this we explained and discussed in *The Illusion of Education* and *The Illusion of School.* However, this pressure has forced students to now seek assistance from AI to provide them with easy solutions to the questions and tasks given to them by their teachers. Recent studies of students using AI have raised a number of concerns we all need to be aware of.

To begin to discuss these, we need to know that a term has now arisen in education known as digital dependency disorder or DDD. This condition arises when a student, for whatever reason, is unable to obtain a response from AI when they are in a competitive environment.

Faced with the concern that other students will find the answer faster and better because they can access AI when they cannot, some students have exhibited serious levels of frustration. Teachers, I am told, have noticed mood swings in children and even violent outbursts through this frustration.

The second and by far the more serious concern relates to a decline in thinking ability. A number of studies have recently shown that students are beginning to decline in their cognitive skills through the use of AI.

One study of high school students who had access to ChatGPT while learning to do math problems showed that they scored lower in tests compared to students who did not have access to ChatGPT. It was simply that students were asking ChatGPT for the answer and were not building the skills that otherwise come through learning to solve problems by themselves.

Two other points of concern arose from this study. First, it was realized that ChatGPT was sometimes found to give wrong responses. Accordingly, its arithmetic computations were wrong eight per cent of the time, but in its step-by-step approach to solving a problem, it was wrong 42 per cent of the time.

The problem here is with students completely trusting AI and not realizing that it only responds with the information it has collected. In earlier stages, AI was fed reliable data, but since then, it has been programmed with questionable data, which it has not been able to recognise as false and thereby combines all in its response to questions. This further adds to a student's frustration when they have not learnt to double-check the information they are provided by AI and so fail in the competition they feel they are in with other students.

In *Reimagining Education in the AI Era,* we saw how university students are taught to reflect on the justification of knowledge, and so are less likely to trust AI-generated information.[1] However, this is not so for students at the school level who do trust AI-generated knowledge, simply because they are purposely deprived of the education in their reason. Why this is so, we explain in *The Illusion of School,* and so why the actual purpose of school is to prepare future citizens to be either managers or managed and not to simply teach children how to learn as we so believe.

Yet, the bottom line to this, as Barzilai discovered, is that a student's ability to reason does not evolve by using AI information to questions they ask. They find the answer, but not how the answer was engineered and so are deprived of the experience in learning how develop their own line of thinking, which returns us to the point we have just discussed. Our students, our future working generation, are learning to think less!

Secondly, the use of ChatGPT was found to cause some students to be overconfident. They believed that they were smarter because they had gained faster responses from AI. It is rather that they think they are a part of AI and so superior by this. Students, for instance, said they did not think that ChatGPT caused them to learn less even though it had. Consequently, it was found that students who had used the AI Tutor thought they had done significantly better on the test, when they had done much worse.[2]

Another study more clearly showed the effect of students using or relying upon AI to help them with their studies. It was found that students desired to use ChatGPT to solve their questions quickly and wanted the right information to gain higher grades. However, using ChatGPT was found to increase their uncertainty in making decisions. Students, in fact, became indecisive because they had become too dependent upon AI to tell them what and how to think.

Another point is that they also tended to easily forget the information they had gained from AI. Thus, the information they gained from AI only served for that moment in time, which gave them too little learning experience. In turn, this affected the development of their memory networks. This study, like others, discussed how students ability to think declines through the use of AI information, rather than improves.[3]

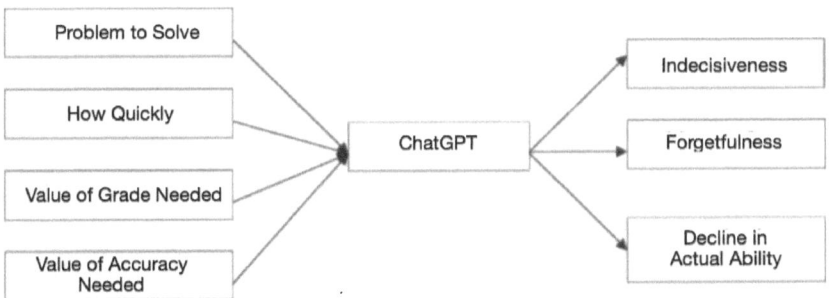

The importance of these two studies shows us why teaching our students how to think and how to reason on their own is now more essential in their education than it ever has been before.

We will return to the effect of AI on the learning process later in our book, but for now let us move to understand how we can help our students to learn to think better and to have higher levels of reason. This will be most important if they are to create the harmonious societies that AI will demand. As we have well painted the picture in other books, our future societies will eventually be administered by AI, which will have little patience with uncontrolled human behavior. Schools must take a new perspective to their purpose.

Indeed, it was for this very reason that this book was written, for it will show you how learning in school is not rocket science. Any child born with normal mental ability can gain the highest marks in a class and top grades in any examination if, but only if, they keep up with the steady buildup of rules upon which the information of school work is based.

It is not, as we shall find, that intelligence enables a student to understand their lessons and gain grades. It is rather that by learning to think through school that a student gains their intelligence. However, what needs to be understood here is that few students learn to really understand how to learn in school, because too few teachers know or teach the way school really works. I will now explain a great secret about school that took me many, many years to discover.

School has created codes by which information may be learned and understood. These codes take the form of two languages. There is the language of mathematics and the national language that is used by the school. For example, in India, they may use English as the medium for communication, rather than one of the many languages of their country. These two languages of school build up very gradually in complexity by their own rules.

For example, in mathematics, just as with physics and chemistry, rules tell the student how to transpose numbers to work out a calculation. If they know the rule, the equation is easily solved. But the problem is that too many students have practiced too few of the rules that lead to a point in time and by this struggle to work with it and so fail to gain competence. Let me give you a very simple example of how easily this happens and of the consequences because of it.

Consider the following sum.

$$6/2\ (2+1) =$$

We will look at two students of completely equal intelligence to see why one appears to be more intelligent than the other.

The student Lara, was listening to the teacher when he explained to the class the rule of BODMAS. This rule requires the student to do the brackets first, then work from left to right as they follow the order to divide, multiply, add, or subtract numbers. She listened and practiced this rule to become proficient with it. So, in finding the answer to this question, Lara did the brackets (2+1) to obtain 3. She then followed the order by dividing 6 by 2 to get 3, and then, she multiplied 3 by 3 to give the answer of 9, which is correct.

However, the student Mark was thinking about other things when the teacher was explaining this rule, and so was not really listening. Again, he may have been sitting in a row too far back from the teacher and could not clearly relate his mind to what the teacher was trying to explain. We will come back to this very important point when we discuss the arrangement of desks in other books..

The point here is that, for whatever reason, Mark missed the rule. Because he did not know of this rule, he used logic to solve the problem.

First, he did the brackets (because he heard this part of what the teacher said) and so got 3 by adding 2 to 1. But, the order to work from the left he did not hear, and so he used common sense by adding this 3 to the 2 to get 6. Then, he divided 6 by 6 to get 1.

Now, the answer One is completely wrong. Mark failed this operation not by his lack of intelligence but by not moving through the rules correctly, but his problem does not end there.

As Mark builds up one misunderstanding or error upon another, his performance will be less than that of others in the class. In turn, he will less believe in himself and so fail to observe information precisely.

He will develop less proficient memory networks and so struggle to remember facts. In other words, his ranking in the class will not be very high, and since he could not respond with the right response and level of confidence to a question asked by the teacher, Mark will be thought to have less intelligence to Lara and other students who 'always' seem to give the right answer.

I will use this example of BODMAS again in our story of Ben, because it so simply illustrates how easily a student fails to understand what they are being taught and so keep up with the progression of their lessons, which ultimately decides their grades in school, and so eventually their opportunities in life.

All we say here for the rules of the language of Mathematics is exactly so for the rules of the language used in the educational system, whether this be English, German, or Japanese. The effort that the student puts into learning the rules:

- of how to spell a word,

- how to construct a sentence correctly (grammar and syntax), and

- how to tell a story. The way they present their mind, either verbally or in writing, will determine the marks they will gain.

This is so right throughout the academic structure, from preschool to advanced degrees. Evaluation in the academic world is only about how well the individual knows how to present information, and how they have learnt to find it or to have developed good memory structures to retain it.

Solving problems is simply a matter of a long chain of experiences with different applications that brought insight. The more emotionally interested the mind is in something, the more it devises ways to associate to this in the memory banks and so can link new information to this to better relate to what it is and the possible meaning to it.

All of this relies upon the individual developing competence with the rules of academia. Consider, now, how learning the rules of a language, and practicing them to become proficient with the use and order of them, greatly determines the ability of the student.

When the Student Learns and Practices the Rules, they:

- Can negotiate through a learning task.
- Have high confidence.
- Interested to explore by themselves.
- Will ask questions more.
- Will interact more and share thoughts more.
- Be interested to remember knowledge.

- They will develop better neural efficiency.
- Feel Inspirational.Be more creative and will carry the skills from this subject into other areas and develop high academic performance.
- Get Good Marks/Grades.

However, when the Student Does Not Learn and and does not Practice the Rules, they:

- Feel lost in negotiating through a learning task.
- Low Confidence.
- Be dependent on others guiding them.
- Will be reluctant to ask questions.
- Will be passive.
- Be little interested and develop poor memory.
- They will be causal in how they identify with information.
- Have no interest in the subject.
- Think the subject is boring and have little interest.
- Get Poor Marks/Grades.

The importance of understanding the value of rules in a student's learning cannot be overemphasised. The student's competence with rules does explain why they vary in their performance in a class.

Thus, a student's performance is not decided by their intelligence or natural ability. It is the more often by the skill of the teacher to generate a desire for the student to want to keep up and to help them to believe in themselves to create the confidence for the student to take their control over their own learning. After all, the top students in a class, those who always gain the highest marks, are those who taught themselves.

School is rules, and how well the child is prepared for these by their home before they enter this system, and how they can then concentrate and work with each, as each is disclosed to them, much decides their performance. According to the grade with which the school rewards them for their compliance, each child will leave this institution to take up a working role and serve their society, either as a manager or as a managed.

- This is school. This is how it works, and this is its purpose!

The purpose of this book is to demonstrate very clearly to a parent, to a teacher, and especially to a student who may find this book interesting, how any child, any student, can move from the bottom of the class to the top. I did, and in many senses, this is my life's story.

So, as we move through this short book, we see how one simple incident lights a spark, and from this, our hero becomes determined to move from being one of the worst in his class to being the best. How Ben manages this reveals how school learning actually happens and so how any student in real life can achieve what Ben does. I, like Ben, learnt to play the rules of the game.

The story of Ben is the story of most children in school, whether their names be Pyotr, Morton, Muhammad, Tenju or Chandra. They are just human children learning to survive in a world they do not understand.

Ben's Story

Ben was late for school. It was not something new. His father worked away from home, and his mother was a nurse working night shift, so Ben had to wake himself up and somehow rouse himself in time to wash, dress, eat breakfast, and catch the bus to school. Something usually went wrong in this sequence of activities. Either he did not hear the alarm bell, which really was a complete disaster, or he would forget his tie when dressing or overindulge himself with Coco Pops and spill milk onto his shirt. Any of which would cause him to miss the school bus.

Then, again, the bus could be slightly early, and even though he would close the house door on time, Ben sometimes glimpsed the tail end of the bus as it disappeared around the corner. The wait for the next bus enviably put him in the bad book, as he was so usually informed by the tight-lipped teacher who stood at the school gate waiting for the last of the late students, before he could lock it and go and get his coffee.

Mr Collins was as furious as ever when Ben entered the classroom to present a new excuse he had worked out on the bus. Matilda smirked at him in her usual way as he moved past her. Matilda was top in the class, always knew the answer, always sat near the teacher's desk and was the most hated in the class, especially by Ben and his pal George. George smiled a welcome as Ben sat next to him at the back of the class.

"What happened?" asked George in a low voice.
Ben merely shrugged his shoulders and started to copy what George had so far written in his exercise book.

Mr Collins was busy writing on the board. The lights reflected off the board, and Ben could not clearly see what he was meant to copy. He did his best. Well, he thought he did. Suddenly, Matilda raised her hand. She always liked to raise her hand as if to show everyone that she was there and the cleverest in the class. Alice, who sat next to her, was more liked by the class. She always seemed to struggle to understand what she should do and had linked herself to Matilda, hoping some of Matilda's brilliance might rub off on her. It never did.

After all, Matilda knew how to stay on top and would only help Alice when she felt it would not lower her status in the class. Judy Green had let it be known to everyone that Alice once had told her, in confidence, that Matilda used to go to a private school. A really posh place, where she got private teachers. Well, that was until her dad's business went bust.

Mr Collins, or rather Old Floppy on account of his uncombed hairstyle that too often resembled a mop that had been stuck on his head, turned from the board to ask a question. He pretended to look at the back of the class, but all knew he was waiting for Matilda to raise her hand and give him the most perfect answer. She did.

Ben watched the scene from the back of the class. *"How does she do it?"* he wondered. *"How does this stuck-up girl always give the right answer faster than anyone else? And why are her marks the highest in the class?"* Ben's marks seldom moved up from the average and more commonly fell below it. Last year, he was 28 in a class of 30 in mathematics. Matilda, of course, was 1st.

It was at that very moment that a thought came to Ben that would change the course of his whole life. He decided that tomorrow, he would come to school very early, earlier than anyone else, and sit in Matilda's seat. He would challenge her! The boy from the back row, always late and whose work was always returned to him with more red ink marks than the black ink he wrote in, would sit in the front of the class.

This, of course, was a very risky thing for him to do. In the back of the class, he could more easily disappear in the mass of other students when asked a question he did not know how to answer. But, stuck out in the very front, this would be a different thing. Here, everyone would laugh at him if he never got things right.

Actually, this thought played on his mind. How could he always give the right answer? Matilda was the cleverest in the class. He knew it, even if he did not want to admit it to himself. She naturally would hate him and snarl at him from the chair she could take. For sure, she would try to humiliate him in any way she could, to prove she is the best and should never be challenged.

"I need a plan," thought Ben. He thought, for a moment, a very brief movement, that he would be Alexander the Great or Napoleon about to launch a military campaign. He might even be the greatest chess player in the world, working out a strategy to checkmate his deadly opponent. This, he thought, was more to the truth, but how could he begin? Better not act tomorrow, he decided. He would plan his move carefully.

This, he was to find out, was the wisest thing he could have done.

That evening, instead of watching TV after dinner and doing his homework at the same time, he went to his room and carefully studied the assignment he had been given. It is not that he never studied any work before, but this time he really thought about the questions in front of him and how he could best answer them.

Ben remembered the movie *The Book Thief*, and somehow the idea came into his mind that instead of just answering the question, he was actually telling a story. It was his story. Not a "once upon a time" type of story, but a story that had a clear beginning, a simple introduction about what he was going to write about. After this, he would plan in sections the thoughts of his story.

The secret of getting good marks, he was learning, is to give lots of facts and weave them into a story. A story that clearly explains what he is going to write about, then does so in clear points, and finishes with a brilliant ending. "Always, think of a great punch line," he remembered some character in a movie explaining.

Actually, it was while he was watching a movie that Ben realized how everyone's brain must be different from everyone else's. So, instead of just sharing his thoughts, he had to visualize how the mind of the person he was writing his story to was blank. It was kind of that their mind had nothing in it. Just an empty space, which he had to fill with his mind, by describing things in a simple and clear order.

Once he began to think like this, Ben found that he became better at explaining his thoughts to others. It became a kind of game for him to think of something complicated, but to explain it in a simple way. As Ben practiced doing this, he found he could make the same great quality of presentations in Geography, History, and even in a Physics write-up. They were all linked to language, and not the entirely different subjects he had always thought they were.

The problem was how to remember the facts. This was not easy. There were always so many. Yet, he remembered how Matilda always managed to do this. She always gave lots of facts. *"I will learn to do the same,"* he said to himself, determined that she was not going to be better than him anymore.

Once he had grasped the importance of this, Ben decided to start making a list of things he should remember from each lesson in each subject. He could not go back to the beginning of the year, and certainly not from the very first time he started school, that was too long ago.

So, he decided only to go over the last three lessons and to build up from there. *"Later on, once I get into the rhythm,"* he thought to himself, *"I can always go back to earlier lessons."* In fact, this is exactly what Ben found himself doing, once he had caught up with the meaning of the lesson he was in.

As he went over things he had earlier learnt, or thought he had learnt but found out he really had not learnt them very well, Ben wondered if there was some special way of remembering things. *There must be some way of linking information together, so the thought of one would trigger off thoughts of another.* He said to himself.

The trouble was that there was always so much to remember, and it was never given to him in any clear way that he could see how one thing linked to another. So, it was that after the lesson, Ben went up to the teacher and asked this question.

"Sir, there are lots to remember and I can't remember them," and added, "Well, not much of them".

Old Floppy, who really was a very kind and patient man, looked at Ben with a sense of admiration for the step the boy was taking to learn how to learn. He waited until the class had been cleared and then explained to Ben how a MindMap worked, and how facts could be associated together to trigger off the memory recognition that Ben was searching for.

The boy's eyes widened with excitement as he listened, questioned, and afterwards began to practice in his mind all the things that Old Floppy had been telling him. Suddenly, Ben began to think that being clever was not something you were born with, as Matilda liked to brag, but only some way of organizing systems of thinking that could be designed and improved upon.

That night, Ben began to Google everything he could find about how to remember things. He found some really good tips from YouTube presenters and really understood more and more how he could become "clever," and certainly cleverer than Matilda.

A plan was forming in his mind how to unthrone Matilda, but not in an unpleasant way. More as a way of showing others in the class how they too could get better marks. He began to see himself as a self-styled savior of his friends in the class. *"He would become a champion for the rights of all,"* he thought to himself, *"just like Robin Hood."*

The effectiveness of reading about something and listening to others talking about how to do something, Ben now realized, was dependent upon how much he altered his own mind.

If he was not fully concentrating, he got a half understanding. But, when he stopped to think about it and related this to something he had remembered in his past, he seemed to remember it better and a lot clearer. It was, as Old Floppy had told him, "Be more sensitive in how you interact with information and the more readily your brain will rewire itself."

Rewire the brain was something new to Ben. Not that he knew anything about how the brain worked. Although in a strange kind of way, he was beginning to understand how brain cells linked together through experience and could change their linking in totally different ways to make you become cleverer.

What Old Floppy also told Ben is that everything in life is related to how sensitive we interact with it, and this is totally dependent upon our emotional state. Be calm but alert, feel happy, and look for something unexpected in information, and you will find it.

Sit in the back of the class and copy, and you don't really learn much at all. It is the interaction, the questioning, the search for relationships with what you know, to what is presented, that is when learning really takes place. Plus, he was told to explain to others what he had learnt, and this would help his brain remember things better.

Ben didn't feel really confident to explain to others, even his best friend George, what he was learning. So, he would go for a walk where no one could hear him and imagine he was talking to someone. It worked. In fact, he got quite good at talking to himself, although he never told anyone he did this. He just felt he became better at explaining things, and the more he did this, the more he remembered things too. He was learning how to tell a better story. All this, Ben kept to himself.

Ben's math teacher was a bit tough. He had been a sea captain and liked to think his students were his sailors, or so the class thought, having nicknamed him Captain Ahab from the movie Moby Dick.

"Here we go for another keel hauling", George whispered to Ben as the teacher walked into the classroom, late as usual. With a stern look around to make sure all his crew were paying full attention, Ahab began to talk about equations and how everything on one side of the equal sign had to have the same value on the other side. John Williams, sitting in the middle, raised his hand and, when given permission to speak, asked, "Does this mean that if we put a whale on one side, we would have to put a whale on the other side too, Sir?"

Mr Jones, this was his real name, nodded and wondered to himself why so many of the class were sniggering to themselves, until Ann Brown put her hand up to go to the toilet, but all knew why she had to leave the room, as she burst into a squeal of laughter just as she reached the door.

Mr. Williams, with a puzzled expression on his face, turned to the blackboard and wrote the letters BODMAS, in large letters. "Rules", he began, "are what all maths is about. Learn the rules and you will sail through maths with no problem. Same with all your other subjects too. Learn the rules of grammar and syntax in English, or Chinese for that matter, if you are in China, and how to tell a good story, and you will get good marks. Don't learn them and you will never understand why you don't".

Ann Brown came back into the room, biting her lip, and sat down. George winked to Ben and both smiled.

So, started Mr. Williams again, or rather Ahab, 'When you are working through a sum, you must follow the rules of BODMAS. First, you do the brackets...." Just as he said this, Ben, for a reason he could never understand, suddenly fell off his chair.

Perhaps it was because he was leaning back against the wall, but he had a suspicion George lifted a front leg up with his foot. All turned at the crash and Ahab shouted so loud, everyone knew he really must have been a sea captain. Once Ben had resumed his sitting position, Ahab continued to tell the class the rest of the rules. Turning back to the board, he wrote the equation 6/2 (2+1) = ?and asked the class to find the answer.

George looked at Ben, and Ben looked at George; neither had a real clue about what to do. But, Ben thought about Matilda and thought he must beat her to the answer. So, George did as he had heard and did the brackets. He added 2 to 1 and got 3. Then, he did the next logical thing: he multiplied 3 by 2 to get 6, then divided 6 by 6 to get 1.

He was about to shout out "Finished, Sir", when Matilda shouted out before him. "The answer is 9, Mr. Williams." Matilda did not turn around to see the faces sneering at her from the rest of the class. She was only interested on Mr.

William's, who congratulated her for getting the right answer.

Nine, thought Ben, *how could it be? The answer is one.*
George looked down at Ben's work and decided to copy it, just in case Mr. Williams would ask him to show his work. *"Nine?"* queried Ben to George. *"The answer is one."*

"So, who got the answer of one?" asked Mr. Williams, with a smile on his face.

Neither Ben nor George moved. It was safer to be at the back of the room, especially if you got the wrong answer and Ahab had that very special smile. The smile that all knew came just before he ordered a sailor to be whipped, or at least they imagined he would have been.

How did she do it? wondered Ben. *How did she get the right answer?*

Alice, sitting next to Matilda, raised her hand. "I also got Nine, Sir." But all knew, even Ahab, that Alice must have copied from Matilda. She usually did.

Suddenly, Ben felt his hand rise. He did not know why it rose. He had no idea he had intended to put his hand up, but once it was up, it seemed to stay up all by itself.

Mr. Williams looked at Ben. "What is it, Ben?" he asked.
Ben felt his throat swallow. It was a very hard swallow. A bit like he had swallowed a big plum, but it was too late. His hand was up, and Ahab wanted to know why.
Ben said, "I got one."

Everyone looked back at Ben, even George looked wide-eyed.

Then, Ahab did a very strange thing. "Well done Ben," he said. "It takes courage to admit when you are wrong. Now, let me tell you why you got one, because I know … I told you to follow the rules, but you did not, Ben".

Ben did not see the others in the class. He was looking at Mr. Williams, whom he suddenly felt great respect for, and was listening hard.

"You heard me say do the brackets first, but you did not listen to the rest of what I was saying."

Actually, Ben, and George too if the truth be told, seldom listened much to what the teacher was talking about. There were other things more interesting, like the movie they watched last night or the new game Ben's father told him he would buy when he next came home.

"What is the next rule?" Mr. Williams asked the class.

Matilda stuck her hand up. In fact, everyone was convinced there was some sort of spring mechanism in her arm that made her hand shoot up so fast, before anyone else's.

"You must work from the left, Sir, and not the right. Then, you do the division, multiplication, addition, and subtraction in that strict order."

"Well done, Matilda", said Mr. Williams. Although Ben was wondering how she knew. He thought about what Mr. Williams had said, that the secret to success is doing the rules.

Ben bit his lip and hated himself for not listening to what Mr. Williams had said. He got it wrong because he had not followed the rules. Because he did not really listen to what he was being told to do, Matilda beat him.

Ben made a promise to himself that he would listen to all the teacher was saying in the future and if he did not understand, then, he would ask for clarification. *No longer will that girl get the right answer before me,* he promised to himself.

George was drawing his pet dog in his exercise book and was lost in his own thoughts. Ben looked at his friend, *I'll help George too* he thought. *From now on, we will listen to all the rules. If,* as Ahab had said, *rules are the way to success, then we will be successful.* As he thought this, he started to wonder what the rules are in English.

A few weeks went by and Ben could not get out of his mind what Mr. Williams had said about rules. Ben had understood why understanding rules are important in math. He had learnt the hard way that they were the secret of getting things right with numbers. In fact, he found that this also worked with the formulas he had to work through in science and physics. He felt a little proud of himself to see more ticks appearing on his sums instead of crosses.

George still got the crosses, and Ben tried to hide the better marks he was given from his friend, so as he would not feel hurt. Ben liked George. They had been friends for a long time. Whenever he went to play in George's house, his mother always made a fantastic cake. "My mother's from

Brazil", George once told him, and Ben had ever since wondered if all cakes in Brazil tasted so good.

But how could rules be important in English, Ben wondered. After all, there were no numbers to move about. You just wrote things down or read about what other people had written down. Ben's English teacher had a wonderful name. He was called Peter Bollodango. He was really nice and everyone loved him. "Bollo" was the name he was called by the other teachers.

In fact, when he first began the year, Mr. Bollodango had told everyone that he loved to teach and that the most important thing was that they should all trust and respect each other. He had said, "You can call me Bollo, everyone does." It seemed strange to call a teacher out loud by a nickname. No one ever dared to do this with Captain Ahab or even Old Floppy, but somehow it seemed very natural to do it with this teacher.

Bollo was not stiff and angry like the other teachers. He was always smiling and happy. And, he taught in a very different way. Ben could always remember a week after Bollo had started, and in coming into the classroom, found the desks laid out around the walls, like a huge U shape. Everyone wondered what was going to happen, since the usual rows and rows had disappeared.

When Bollo began to teach, he did not stand near the blackboard and just talk and talk, and talk like Old Floppy. Instead, he did a very curious thing. Bollo would walk within the U shape, like he was an actor on the stage. He would say something and get you to think about it.

Ben found that with the desks arranged like this, he kind of felt he was alone with the teacher. It kind of gave him the confidence to ask questions. The thing was, was that Bollo did not give you the answer, but he asked a question in return that helped you to see the answer yourself. Ben liked Bollo. They all did. He even allowed you to eat and drink during the lesson. "If the brain is going to work", he had said, "it needs energy."

"Why?" asked Polina, whose parents came from Russia. She was smart like Matilda but did not show off. Everyone liked Polina and wondered if her parents had been famous. Her father was known to play the violin, but she never bragged about anything and generally kept herself to herself. Ben liked her.

Bollo asked her in return, as he usually does, "Tell me, Polina, how does a cell get energy to metabolize?"

"It needs sugar and oxygen," she replied.

"So," said Bollo, "are we not just cells, billions and billions of them all glued together? So, as they need sugar, which you get from eating, you need oxygen. This is why I allow you to move about when I am talking." He paused for a moment when he said this to give a smile mixed with a frown at Aussie. Aussie was from Australia and had tried to climb out of the window when Bollo said be free in my class. But Bollo had that certain way that no one really wanted to escape from his lessons. Aussie had only been joking.

It was during one lesson that Ben put his hand up. In fact, all students did this with Bollo, when they had something on their mind, even George. Bollo looked at Ben, inviting him to talk.

"How does English have rules?"

"Rules! Well, they are the things that make everything possible," replied Bollo, who then explained in a story-like way, how rules join letters to make words, and gave the example of where and were. This was really interesting, because Ben had always gotten these words mixed up. But Bollo then went on to explain how rules place words in the correct order in a sentence. Bollo loved to tell things as a story. It always made listening to him so interesting.

Ben had never thought of rules to explain spelling. He wrote as he thought, without knowing there was a science behind it. It was the same with a sentence. He just did it his way, but Bollo had caused Ben to think more about how he was spelling words and how verbs and nouns and adjectives and all the other stuff actually all played a part together.

Most interestingly, Bollo had asked Ben if he knew what was on his mind. Ben shook his head. *How could he?*

"So", explained Bollo, "then you must be very clear about giving your thoughts to me. I need you to tell me what you are going to give me.

Not in a long and complicated way. Just a short way, so I can pull my mind around what you are going to say. Call it an introduction if you like. Once I have opened my mind to yours, then tell me your story. Do it in short sections to make sure I can keep up and then finish off with a loud bang".

He demonstrated this by bringing his big hands together, making a big clap. Bollo loved to be an actor, and Ben and all the others loved to be his audience. Lessons were always fun and meaningful. "The ending, your ending, is where you give the meaning of what your story was all about. So make it a great one. A great ending makes a great story."

Ben had realized that Bollo was telling them all a secret. A secret that no other teacher had told them, except for what Ahab had said. But now Ben realized how he could get better marks. He just had to learn all the rules that made up English, as well as maths. *There must be lots of them,* thought Ben, and he felt a bit sorry that no teacher had explained this to him when he first began school. But that was a long time ago, and nobody then had any idea they would come to learn things.

School was just a place they had to come to. "Jail for life", George had once said. Ben was beginning to think school could not really be like jail, especially with a teacher like Bollo. He liked this teacher and had already decided that he would change things the way he did. After all, this was necessary if he was going to beat Matilda. Actually, he had noticed that in Bollo's class, Matilda did not seem so stuck up, a bit more like the rest. He was not sure why, and suspected she was working on some kind of master plan to destroy the world.

"Who was the greatest genius?" Mr.Flynn, the physics teacher, asked Ben. Ben had no idea. He was not even sure what a genius was, but around the walls of the physics room were lots and lots of pictures of Einstein.

"Einstein! replied Ben, not really sure.

"Yes. Yes. Of course, he was, but do you know why?"
Ben had no idea.

"Well, he was not born that way, he learnt how to be a genius."

"How can you learn to be a genius, Sir?" Ben had never thought about this before.

"Einstein learnt the 3 P's. persistence, perseverance, and passion."

"That's all?" inquired Ben, a little bit confused.

"Yes, of course, it is, boy. The three P's and never forget them. Persistence, Perseverance and Passion."

Ben lay in bed that night thinking about this. If Einstein could learn to be a genius, then so could he. Ben fell asleep wondering how he could design a rocket to travel deep into space.

As the days went by, one of the things Ben did that really brought his marks up, and it was a very simple thing, was that he started to check things by himself, before he handed his work to the teacher. It began with Captain Ahab in a rare moment of kindness that always made everyone suspicious of what might come next. As he walked around the class, checking the work of each student, he eventually came to Ben at the back.

"Look, Ben", he said, "even you can find these silly mistakes. Learn to check what you do before you give me your work. If you can spot and correct your own mistakes, you will give me a better paper to mark. Then, I can give you a higher grade." Ben was taken aback by this act of kindness and wondered if Mr. Jones might not be so bad as everyone thought. But, this made sense, and he wondered why no teacher had ever told him this before.

So, Ben started to check each line as he worked through it. It seemed laborious at first, but Ben soon learnt to make his checks quickly and develop a self-checking mind. It paid off. Instead of just working through the sums given to him and waiting for Ahab to hand back his work with red circles here and there and more crosses than ticks, Ben learnt to find his own errors as he worked through each equation.

Then, strangely, he felt more confident. He realized that he could be very good all by himself if he learnt to trust himself more. This, he did by checking. It seemed too simple a thing, but it made a huge difference.

Since this worked in mathematics, Ben saw how it could work in all his other subjects. So, he started to think more about how letters formed words and words formed sentences. As he checked sentences, so he found he could improve their meaning and presentation simply by thinking more about the words he chose. Then, he started to think more about how to make his sentences run into each other better and where to put commas.

The thing was that Ben realized that if he did this in Geography and remembered the things he was taught, his marks in Geography went up. He did the same in History, and his marks went up there. The same was with Science and the most boring of all subjects, Religion.

Grades, Ben came to understand, simply were given according to what he could remember, and he had found good ways to do this, and the way he told his thoughts to create his story. Ben started to read more books and studied how the author created his story. He was learning how to present his mind better.

Yet, somehow, sitting at the back of the class made it more difficult for him to ask Old Floppy a question. Each time he raised his hand, others in the class would look back at him, some would snigger, and others seemed to wait for him to make a mistake. So, Ben avoided asking questions.

Then, he thought, if he was in the very front of the class, he would be much less aware of others knocking his confidence. After all, he wouldn't see them. Then, it struck him. Matilda never cared what others thought about her; maybe she just blocked them out of her mind, because she was right in the front and couldn't see those behind her.

In a way, he never expected, parts of a jigsaw began to come together. He was beginning to see a way he could match Matilda and even beat her to become the best student in the class. He had to sit in the front row.

The trouble was that if he could do this, Matilda would deliberately try to shoot him down, which he didn't feel he had the confidence for. So, either he would sit next to her in a way of trying to needle her, which he would hate to do, or sit far away from her at the end of the row.

That night, Ben prepared for the coming lesson. Ben had learnt to be prepared for the lesson that was coming. He re-read previous lessons, thought about new associations and connections to what he had learnt, to understand them better.

This, he found, really helped him to understand and remember things. In fact, he long ago stopped just walking into the classroom and waiting for the teacher to begin the lesson, as was the usual way for students. Ben would find out what the coming lesson was about and read up on this. He would even search YouTube for anything related to what the lesson might be about. Ben was becoming his own teacher.

As his success in the class began to rise, he realized that Matilda was the best simply because she had long been doing what he was now discovering to do. She was not born any better, but simply had gained a higher confidence in her ability through the better strategies to learn, remember and share her thoughts she had developed.

Ben wondered if it made a difference that her father was an accountant. *Could he have passed on tricks in thinking that helped her to learn better?* When he thought of this, Ben felt a bit sad, because he seldom saw his father, and his mother was always very busy and never found the time to sit down and explain things to him.

Still, Ben was determined to teach himself. He remembered the story of Abraham Lincoln, the greatest president in American history, and how he had taught himself how to think, coming from a poor farming background. Thinking of others who had overcome great obstacles to succeed gave him a sort of belief that he could do the same.

When the lesson began the next day, Matilda sat in the front row full of confidence and ever ready to please Old Floppy. Ben had managed to come earlier to the classroom and had got a seat in the front row, but as far from her as he could manage. George sat behind his friend, wishing him good fortune in the coming battle. The subject was history, and the topic was the 1848 revolutions.

As soon as Old Floppy opened up the lesson, Ben shot his hand up and asked why there had been a succession of revolutions more in Paris than in any other city in Europe. Matilda stirred at him with burning eyes, trying to set him on fire. As the teacher ran off a number of reasons, Ben interrupted him. "But Sir, was it not really a reaction to the government's attempt to control the campaigns designed to destabilize the king's power?"

Old Floppy looked a little taken aback and smiled at Ben encouragingly. Ben could not stop himself from half-turning to Matilda and adding, "And that from this revolution came the words Liberty, Equality, and Fraternity, which are now so famous?"

Matilda blinked uncomprehendingly at where this threat to her position had come from, but Ben was so much now in charge of his own situation that he simply forgot about her presence. In fact, for the first time since he began school so many years ago, he now realized it could be fun.

Matilda, however, saw no fun in Ben outshining her. Desperate to regain her position in front of the class, she saw to outmaneuver him by trying to take the lesson in a different direction, but Ben had well prepared the ground.

Each thrust that Matilda gave was easily parried by Ben, because he had prepared for the lesson and she had not. Or at least, not as well as he had. Feeling she was rapidly losing face, Matilda shouted at Alice for distracting her. Poor Alice looked most upset and was beginning to see a future ally in Ben, because she knew he was kinder.

The bell to end the lesson came too quickly for the class, who were now enjoying the open contest. Some, mostly girls, supported Matilda, but it was Ben who really earned the respect of everyone in the class, including Old Floppy, much to the bitterness of Matilda. She had lost. Ben had won.

The next day, something really strange happened. He had just sat down. Ben was never late now. He liked school; maybe it was just that it did not seem such a bad place after all. He kind of felt it was beginning to feel like home now. The teachers stopped shouting at him, more in the class liked him and he enjoyed asking questions.

It was just near the end of the music lesson that Alice came over to him and passed him a small white envelope. It was not addressed to anyone, but he guessed it was for him. Curiously, he opened it, careful to watch that Miss Smit did not see it as she was arranging the class to put back their instruments. Ben had a drum. It was not a big one, but he liked to make is sound like one.

Inside the envelope was a card. No one had ever given him a card before. Well, of course, mum and dad had when it was his birthday, and Aunt Judy always sent some money with her card. Ben did not expect any money inside the card, but when he opened it, there was something just as good. Written in beautiful writing were the words ..

> You are Great Ben
> M.

Ben looked across at Matilda. It had to be her who sent it. He felt strange. He did not seem to hate her anymore, and he was beginning to wonder if he might really like her after all.

The End

Reflections:

Our story of Ben gives valuable insight into how children learn, how they can learn better and also how school really works. These are factors that many would be very interested to know.

If we look back on our imaginary character Ben, we see a very normal young person. The character, of course, could have been a girl as much as a boy, but the theme of their life would be much the same. They are innocent of the meanings of the world and of the design and ways of the school. They move through their life on the guidance or lack of it they receive from others, as they try to find their place in the scheme of things. All they desire is first to be happy and second to be individually respected in the mayhem of struggling personalities they are forced into every day. For most of them, the meaning of learning in school would come a poor third.

In our story, Ben's father is working away from home, and so is little available to give him a direction in his life. His mother has to work nightshift and so is absent in Ben's mornings. He has to learn to look after himself very early in life. The reality today is that few children gain the loving guidance of both parents, often because they do not know or have forgotten the ways their parents raised them.

Young parents today would have been the product of game playing in their youth, and too often lacked clear directions from their family, which was so important in their development. So, it would seem normal for them to raise their children as they experienced their childhood. We do not mention here the rising impact of drugs or the negative, at times evil, effects of social media that play on the minds of children today.

I would like to share an incident here, which I described in my book *Brain Plasticity,* since it helps us to understand what many parents today do not understand.

" … She'll be starting school soon." I was told by the proud father. The mother standing nearby joined in. "She's already in kindergarten now." Then added, "It's the best private one in our area," as if to reassure me that their daughter was being well prepared for life.

Yet, before they told me this, I had noticed how neither parent on our bus journey had given the slightest attention to their child. Strapped into a wheelchair on a hot summer's day, the little girl was told to stop moving about and not to cry. As one parent sat with headphones on, humming away to the music they were listening to, and the other stared out of the window for the whole length of the journey, both were totally oblivious to the boredom that was self-evident to me on the child's face. A fact, easily witnessed in the way she kept tugging at a strap of the chair, desperate to create some type of stimulation.

Seeing the child's frustration in her face, I made a movement to catch her eye, and as her's caught mine, a smile rose upon her cheeks. She laughed a little as I made a funny gesture, and while I longed to interrupt the parents and explain to them what they did not understand, I felt I had no right to intrude into their private lives.

So, as I tried to stimulate the child's mind with funny gestures and strange actions, I secretly prayed that somehow she might one day be inspired to change the world that was being created for her. However, the more I thought about the child's future, the more encouraged I felt to talk to the parents and politely moved to do so. They were very kind and delighted I had made the effort. It was then, they told me how well she'd do in school.

The problem, as I realized in talking to these parents, is that they believed school was going to teach their daughter. They had no idea that when their child would begin school, it could be too late, as other children had been raised with better skills and prepared with a better frame of mind for what was to come.

Learning is not limited to crayons, paints, pictures, and sounds kindergarten and early school will introduce children to; it is also about acquiring a fine sensitivity in the awareness of things and the relationships they have. It is the acquisition of this sensitivity alongside a high quality of language that is the key to higher learning. This is the job of the parent, but too many little realise what this means.

Those who do will be those who were so raised by their parents, or woken to the urgency of this need by a university education, as we discuss in other books. These young parents had simply no understanding of the need to stimulate the mind of their daughter, or what they could achieve by doing this. They just did not know. ...."

Accordingly, we find too many children lacking clear guidance and who miss clear lines to know what to do and what not to do in how they are responsible to themselves and to others around them. Without this clear orientation in their life, they are seemingly without direction in their studies.

And so, as we found, Ben is quite lost in his world. He drifts through it quite uncomprehending of the direction his life will go after school. He has to go to school. He has no choice. It is the law. We may imagine he would not know what to do otherwise in his life, save to drift in the mind trap of game playing that lures his generation. So, he is told to wake up, dress, eat his breakfast, catch the bus, and once in school, be processed according to the display he makes to the system that daily assesses and ultimately evaluates his worth to the working world.

Without understanding how his time in school is to prepare his life for after school, Ben carries each day as a burden, longing to be free. Like most children, Ben seeks to gain a sense of the freedom he desires by resisting the total control over him that authority demands, until it has transformed him from a carefree child into a responsible citizen who can comply with the rules of work he is given.

Yet, by his small acts of rebellion, Ben fails to be sensitive to the information in his lessons. He does not concentrate, or if he does, it is only half so, and by this he misses the small and crucial rules that enable clear understanding to be gained. Without such knowledge, Ben is confused in what to do when moving through a learning task. Unsure, he will often guess what to do, which will invariably be the wrong guess. He may even try to copy from someone else if he can, simply to give the impression that he knows what he does not and so avoid humiliation in the class — humiliation given total recognition should he put up his hand and ask the teacher for help, again.

So, like most children, Ben struggles through each lesson as mystified at the end as to what he thought he would learn at the beginning and trusts the lesser mark of the teacher, which confirms he did not understand the whole lesson or much of it.

Indeed, the path for Ben seems to be set by his domestic life, geared by the friends he has and fixed to the role he plays in a class of others who also do not want to be there. All that is, until something happens. One event, and this can often be the case, offers Ben a new role in the class, and ultimately a new life scenario after his time in school. Ben does learn how to be smart.

My purpose in writing this short and simple book is to show how any of us can light such inspiration in any child and guide them to know how to reach the highest evaluation. It is not always easy, and often any warnings we give to them if they do not try harder either fall on deaf ears or frustrate them when they try harder and yet fail to gain more recognition by doing so.

Thus, the difference comes, as we saw with Ben, when the desire, the drive to achieve, comes from within. It is only when this occurs that the student searches for themselves and learns through trial and error, by which they discover what is better to do and how to do it. It is this inner drive that fuels the sensitivity that really gives the higher quality that gains the recognition sought. This, however, is too often dampened and destroyed in too many students.

The reality is that learning in school is not simply learning. It is more a competition of minds, with each challenging others for their recognition from the teacher, and with this, the hope of a better mark. It is the drive of the student to keep up, to avoid the multitude of distractions that seek to occupy their thoughts, and to continually check and redefine information through their own understanding of it, that enables each to rise within the class or to fall by their failure to do so.

This is to say that from their earliest times in school, or rather the educational process, students will compete against each other. Some will openly demonstrate this, others will hide it, but all learn very quickly that they are in a game of winners and losers. Teachers may tell them otherwise, but each happily or worryingly sees the marks awarded to those about them and knows the truth. By this continual comparing of their ability with others, each develops a fear of failing. Too common is the comment from a student: "I can't do this."

It is important to understand that the mind of the student is continually trying to organize new information according to how well they have understood similar information before. If they recognise the links easily, they feel confident to engage the task, but if they do not clearly see a link, when they feel others can, a sense of inadequacy grows within them. It is this fear of not being equal in a task that destroys their confidence to believe they can be successful in it. A quiet panic takes over their thinking, which is not witnessed by others, and their mind fails to see the links they are desperate to recognize.

In all the cases I have had of students who did not do well in their classes or did not understand some factor of a lesson, and there have been far more than I could count, it is clear to me that if the teacher wishes to improve a student's understanding or correct some mistake of theirs that they must first create a bond of trust. This is imperative. For this trust, which is based on a sense of human love, conveys to the student a conviction that the teacher can be relied upon to "carry" them through their struggles to understand.

Indeed, it is the function of the teacher to first provide information, and then to explain in a sympathetic manner how this can be better understood by a student who did not concentrate when they first explained it to them, or they have missed, by whatever reason, earlier information that enables this information to be understood.

If there were one teacher for one student, this would be a simple affair, but with one teacher responsible for 30 or so different minds of widely different experiences of life and not just school, each driven by their own interests and insecurities, a vast range of different abilities soon appears within the class of students.

When Ben's mind drifted as his maths teacher was explaining BODMAS, we see how even a fleeting distraction can cause a student to fail to understand a rule to keep up with the flow of knowledge being shared with them.

It is imperative that we understand the significance of this, because when this happens, and it too often does in a class, the student gets stuck when they are negotiating through a task. Reluctant to ask the teacher to explain what they already have and incur some humiliation from others in the class by doing so, the student is likely to copy from someone next to them or guess what to do. This is what Ben did. He missed the rule, and he guessed; unfortunately, it was the wrong guess, and yet this is what happens.

Accordingly, by the struggles of each to fully concentrate or to fail to do so, each obtains a mark for their effort. Yet, this mark is not always easy for them to understand or seem fair. Students often question themselves as to why they did not get a better mark. To understand this, we must always remember that school is a processing system, where the teacher has to show they are doing their job by marking students differently.

Not all students can be given the highest mark, just as not all can be given the lowest. The teacher has to show a range of marks varying somewhat about the average and always showing they are good enough by one or two of their students gaining excellent marks. To try to understand this state of affairs is to take us into a quandary, because it is widely believed that different students have different natural abilities, which is reflected in the different marks each gains, even though this is not so.

To understand this, we should know that a belief arose in the 19th century that intelligence is largely inherited and that it can be measured in the individual, so that a range of intelligences can be set about the average. This is to say that the most of any group measured will have the average ability for intelligence, this is set to a score of 100 in an IQ test, with lesser and greater degrees of ability moving away from this average.

While learning ability in school has nothing to do with intelligence, upon the strategies and circumstances we have examined, the idea arose in the 19th century that it does. This sees the smartest student gaining the highest scores. From this reasoning came the understanding that any assessment of students should naturally be set about an average. This is to say that not all could be given top marks or all given very low marks.

By holding to the belief that student ability, which is to mean intelligence is inherited (to some unknown factor), education seeks to release itself from criticism, when employers complain of the poor capability of new workers or parents complain of the low marks and grades their children gain.

Therefore, while parents may rightly criticize a teacher and even the school, the school has long learnt how to defend itself and its teachers by finding some blame in the child or their circumstances. Therefore, it seems natural to all concerned that the performance or rather ability in a class will vary about the average.

So, the teacher works with the design given to them by factors in education, to set the average mark for their class. In doing this, they must show how the class excels due to the quality of their education and grade one or two students A+ or 10/10 to prove this. However, if they were to show an equal opposite (which would be the true meaning of an average) and mark even one student Z or 0/10, the teacher would be regarded as incompetent. So, class marks vary between 4/10 to 10/10.

Teachers regard the effort of the students to be the student's responsibility and mark assignments accordingly, giving notes of encouragement that little guide a student in how to improve their marks. Thus, a student marked 6/10 may be given the encouragement "Well Done" or "Try harder", neither of which helps the student to understand precisely what they need to do to do better.

One of the greater problems here is that students have long been conditioned to see the teacher as infallible and that the evaluation they give to be correct and must be so. This sets within the mind of the student an acceptance of what they are and what they can be, and so very few learn, as Ben did, that marks do not classify potential. And yet, in having said this, the teacher must make it so, because they have to show a certain regularity in student performance to prove their ability to teach.

Therefore, if one student moves up in this scheme of things, another will be marked down, to maintain a certain range of ability in the class. This fits into the idea of intelligence varying about the average in any group, which gives education an excuse from lack of finances, poor teaching, and low classroom management skills to explain poor student performance. All this is set about the concept of inheritance being naturally inherited, to some extent.

After 40 years of research, I wrote *Intelligence: The Great Lie* to explain how and why the idea we have of an inherited intelligence is wrong, and all that stems from it in the education of the child and the ways adults are assessed for a part to play in the workings of their society.

To do this, I had to go back nearly 200 years to explain how the root of this belief arose to politically counter the rise of socialism in the 19th century. As the cry for equality arose from the lower ranks of society, at that time, claiming that all men are born equal, those at the top and with the most to lose managed to create a mindset that all are not born equal; and that civilized order could only be maintained by the sons following the work and social role of their fathers and those before them.

The Science of Psychology grew from this argument and has attempted ever since to prove that intelligence is inherited and that it can be measured. *Intelligence: The Great Lie* rationally explains why this feature it is not inherited as is believed and certainly not measurable, any more than a thought or a dream.

However, this is unknown to the public at large and little more so to those working within education, as they witness a certain regularity in the efforts and abilities of their students.

And yet, if we move away from this idea of regularity in learning ability as a product of some inborn quality of intelligence, which there is no evidence of in normally born children, we are caused to focus on how each developed and therefore how each could be better developed. We saw many examples of this in our short story of Ben. Quite simply, Ben, taken to be a normal child in school, simply did not know the importance of checking his work or of keeping up with each lesson as one progressed to the next.

This may seem common sense to us, but it was quite unknown to Ben, as it is to virtually all children in school. After all, it makes sense to check what you have done before letting another person evaluate your effort. Yet very, very few children and students at all levels of education, including those at the university level, think to do this. Too many assume that what they have done is the best they can do and are puzzled why others find fault with their work or mark it less than perfect.

So, we find that with a little guidance from "Captain Ahab", Ben starts to check his work as he does it. By doing this, Ben learns to find his own mistakes and so becomes more aware of what he is doing, when he is doing it. As Ben learns to better craft his effort and sees better recognition from his teachers for doing so, his self-confidence improves. As Ben comes to believe more in himself, he puts more effort into thinking about how he can be better.

Within our short story of Ben, we find glimpses of how ability is developed within the school complex, by students understanding or failing to understand each of the many rules that enable them to be proficient.

The example we saw with BODMAS highlights exactly this situation. We may see that just as Ben lost track of the rules the teacher was explaining to him, so how another could lose track of the order of Pythagoras' Theorem $C^2 = A^2 + B^2$ and think it to be $A^2 = C^2 + B^2$, whereby doing so they lose marks.

To understand further how learning and so how evaluation of a student's competence really comes down to how well they learnt the relevant rules, and so nothing about their natural ability, let's look at a very simple question that stumps many students when they were not taught to fully understand the rules involved.

A teacher may argue here that the class were taught the rules, but I know through my experience that unless the rules are drilled into all minds and repeated later, then not all members of the class will know of these rules, or how to use them.

Without knowing the rules, the students become confused about how to solve a question given to them. This confusion is wrongly used to explain the variation of ability in a class and so the range of competence of the students, rather than that of the teacher or the system which controls their efficiency. We shall come back to this later in our short story, but the is factor is much discussed in our book *The Illusion of Education*. Let us consider, then, the question:

"If ten dollars buys 6 sweets, how many sweets can you buy for 15 dollars?"

Now, if the student has not learnt the rules to decode this information, they are easily lost in how to tackle the question. In being, so self-doubt settles in and they feel they can't do it, they can't do maths, and consequently hate maths.

They carry this negative mind into each math lesson, which actually generates a chemical movement in their brain that hinders the flow of signals between neurons, causing them to be insensitive in how they handle information. In turn, this causes them to make mistakes too easily in realizing what information is and how best to process it.

Thus, the secret in all such riddles is to take the numbers out of the wording and see simple relationships. This is to say that ten dollars equals six sweets. Mathematically, this is expressed as

$$10 = 6$$

Now, the next step is to discover how many sweets can be bought for one dollar. However, before we move to this step. There are rules to be known.

The first rule is to know that whatever you do to one side of the equal sign must be done to the other side to maintain balance. If you add 1 or X to one side, you must add 1 or X to the other side, so that the equation is held in balance. This balance is important to know.

The second rule here is to know that when you move a number or a value from one side of the equal sign, it must take the opposite value when it is taken over. Thus, 1 becomes -1, and x10 becomes /10.

With these rules known, the rule to begin the calculation is to multiply each factor on either side of the equal sign by 1.

The rule is to know that anything can be multiplied by 1, which will not change its value. Thus, 1 x 10 is 10.

$$\text{So we see how } 1 \times 10 = 1 \times 6$$
$$\text{becomes } 1 = 6/10$$
$$\text{and so } 1 = 0.6$$

Now, we know that 1 dollar equals 0.6 sweets.
The next step is to find out how many sweets are worth 15 dollars.

If we now follow the rule of adding a number to both sides of the equal sign, we may place 15 on either side of the equal sign, as:

$$15 \times 1 = 15 \times 0.6$$
$$\text{We calculate this to}$$
$$15 = 9$$

So we find the answer that 15 dollars buys 9 sweets.

This is extremely easy once, but only once, all the relevant rules are known and practiced.

The problem, as we have seen throughout this short book, is that not all students in a class paid attention to the rules when they were introduced, or soon forgot them because they did not practice using them.

This is exactly the same principle as the rules for the language of communication used in the school system. How well a student pays attention and practices the rules of spelling, of grammar, of syntax, and learn/loves to express their mind with a clear story context, are the factors used to evaluate their competence.

The facts they weave into "their story" be it for a history or geography assignment, etc, are ones they develop through their interest in the subject, which is much allied to their respect for their teacher and the respect they feel the teacher has for them or their sense of acceptance within those they are forced to learn with.

Let us very briefly now try to understand an educational system that, on the one hand, encourages teachers to do their best to teach their students how to learn, but on the other hand has long devised strategies to compound their abilities, exhaust their energies, and provide sound reasoning why all students cannot learn to be the best in the class.

All of which may cause us to ponder, when the child population is increasing around the world, as to why education has devised strategies that are causing teachers to leave education in their droves. Who, we may question, will be left to teach our children?

The obvious answer is A.I., but as we saw at the beginning of this book, learning through AI reduces the cognitive skills of students. Yet, there is another consideration here, for depriving children of learning through an adult and replacing the adult with an AI tutor also deprives them of developing moral and human skills.

Another Perspective of School

As the rules of one lesson lay foundations for those that follow, it is essential that every student literally fights to keep up. Very few do, of course, much because they do not know how information builds up through a syllabus and have fallen into the trap of thinking the teacher will do the thinking for them. It is only the very few who consistently score high in the class who have learnt the truth about the situation and taught themselves.

Such rules, as we have explained, are essential to working through and solving equations in maths and the science subjects, such as physics, because they are the tools to transpose numbers about and follow a clear mechanism of thought. If the student has not learnt these simple rules, they cannot gain full marks and so fail to be distinguished. They become one of the grey average who struggle to do better, but never understand why they are not at the top of the class.

As we have seen, it is the same with the rules for language, upon which the other subjects of the curriculum are made up, such as History and Geography, etc. How the student expresses their response to questions in assignments and examinations will lie significantly in their skill of language, spelling (knowing the difference between WHERE and WERE, for example), grammar, and the way they present their mind. This is their ability to essentially tell a good story, marked by the quality of language they use.

The recognition they gain through learning these rules inspires within them a certain confidence in how they should be alert when evaluating and processing information. The confidence they have in their belief causes them to be more like a subject they feel they are good at. In turn, this causes them to be more sensitive in the handling of their information, which causes them to better understand it, gain better marks, and so feel more confident. Everything centres around the student's competence with the rules of the two languages, but this is seldom, if ever, explained to the students.

As we may now understand, it is not that students are clever or not so. It is simply a question of the language skills they have through the rules they have striven to keep up with and the facts they can pull in to give their story meaning. If one infant were to write " The sun is hot" and another "The sun is big, yellow, and hot," we know who will gain the greater recognition by their teacher.

The principle is the same throughout education. Marks and grades come down to the quality of language the student is able to express their mind with, plus the facts they weave into their story to make it more relevant.

Thus, assessment in education comes down to a skill in language, the effort for attention, and to practice, from different perspectives, what they have learnt to be competent with. The more effort they engage in the learning process, the more tuned their brain will become to identifying, processing and recognizing the meaning of information.

The learning of facts, as can be witnessed with Mind Maps, is simply learning to organize information to be recalled. The more funny, the more outlandish the student can make a fact, the more they will remember it. This can be related to how happy and secure they feel with the teacher and those they must learn with. As they strive to learn more, with sensitivity that is, the better their brain becomes at recognizing, storing, and evaluating information.

Thus, how well a student remembers the facts, which they weave into their responses and answers, much determines the grades they earn. Their desire to keep up with the increasing progression of rules and the facts of the subject they are expected to remember too often lies in the interest they have in the subject and with the teacher of this subject. Too often, a student will remark, "I hate maths," and shortly later add, "I hate the teacher," or "I love my teacher, I love maths."

We see here how the transmission of information is related to the learner's perspective of those involved with this transmission. Learning is not simply about facts, but about human interaction, and this is never more so than in education. Despite the efforts of the good teacher, many students fail in their learning not because of their inability, but because they are distracted from understanding and interacting with their learning by others around them.

Despite the good intentions of many adults, to the child in school, it still remains a survival of the fittest. This may not seem so, as the teacher casts their eyes over the 30 or so beaming faces staring back at them. Yet, if they could go into any one of those minds, they would see it to be a chaotic circus of doubts and insecurities seeking to know how best to be accepted by those about them and the teacher who seals their fate with the red marks they sprinkle over the perfect work they believe they have handed in. There again, and as we shall soon discover, school was never meant to be anything other than a weeding out process.

As the personalities of students conflict and the insecurities of some seek to show to others a bolder facade, bullying occurs. While this has always been a factor of school life, few really understand what it means to the victim.

A great friend of mine in the U.S, Rusty May devotes his energies to educating school children about the dangers of bullying and teaching victims how not to be so. (If you have any concerns relating to bullying, please do contact Rusty at https://schooltoolstv.com.)

In many of our other books, we go beyond discussing the psychological dangers of this to explain how bullying alters the chemical arrangement of the victim's brain and how this affects their personality, self-confidence, and ability to keep focused in their learning.

Although this process is described in detail in *Brain Plasticity: How the Brain Learns through the Mind to Create Intelligence,* we may know here that a teacher humiliating a student, another student attacking their social identity, and not just physically injuring them, can cause a hormone called cortisol to rise in their brain. As cortisol rises, it blocks parts of the brain trying to deal with how to understand a learning task or problem.

This rise of cortisol causes the brain to direct the attention of the mind to focus on the danger (the bullying student, the threatening teacher), and so be distracted from the learning process. This may occur for a fleeting second, but it is more likely to disrupt the victim's learning for a few lessons and, in some cases, extend throughout the whole year, depending upon how they learn to overcome the threat to them.

I have never met one teacher who has heard of the effect of cortisol or knew how detrimental it is to the learning development of the students they are responsible for. Yet, it is vital that all teachers know of this and know how to prevent its occurrence in their students by keeping their minds fully active, full of fun, and absorbed in the information they are sharing with them.

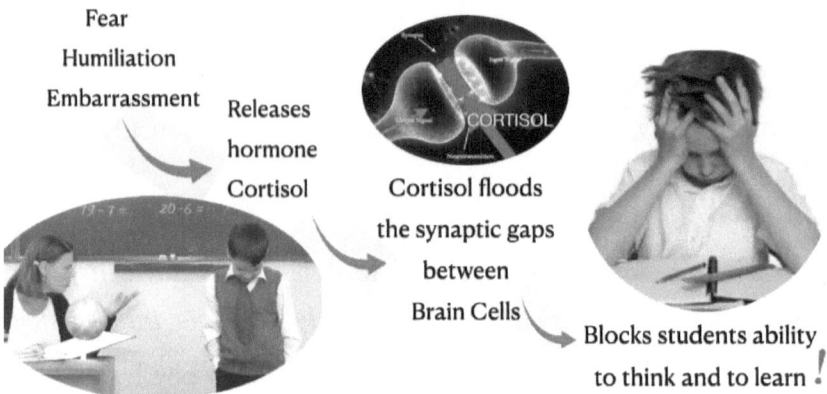

It is not, then, that the teacher is there to give information, as some teachers but certainly not all think is their purpose, but to inspire the minds of all of their students to believe in themselves and to engage in their learning with a happy and attentive mind. This is the real skill of a good teacher, as Ben discovered.

This leads us to ask how we, as educationalists and parents, may better improve in our guidance to the young we are responsible to. For the educationalist, the teacher doing the job, this is for them to juggle with information in a manner that keeps the minds of each student fully focused on them while they teach the lesson. This is not an easy thing to accomplish.

However, I have designed a method of teaching whereby the teacher can largely keep the attention and understanding of the full class through the entire duration of a lesson. I give an introduction to this on the last pages of this book, but active details of this method are explained in other books, namely *Teach*

Better, Learn Better, and centre about what I call a *Sensitivity in Awareness.*

Such *Sensitivity in Awareness* is a skill that any educationalist or parent can master. It is not inborn. It develops through the life experiences of the individual. It may be passed on in facets of guidance as one individual shares moments with another and it grows within the individual through the empathy they have for others and/or the depth of interest they have in pursuing an ideal. As such it is an art. It is not one that is studied in education, but it should be for it underlies all learning processes.

The education of *Sensitivity in Awareness,* in my opinion, should form part of a subject in the curriculum, because it raises the student above the domestic thinking skills they use in school. It is one of the means by which equality in learning and in thinking and, of course, in reasoning can be achieved.

It is not, then, the quality of genes a student inherits that determines how they fare in education, but by three definite factors we have identified:

- How well they keep up with the rules of the two languages.

- How they are able to control their mind to offset distractions.

- The purpose they have to want to succeed in their learning.

So, it is not just that each student gains a mark for what they are worth. It is that each student is marked within all others, as they can show the skill they have developed through the innumerable rules they have given attention to know and then practiced to be proficient with it.

This is all academic proficiency is. It is simply a matter of skills. Some learn these early, some never do. Ben, we saw, got lucky.

In our simple story, we find the real cause of differences in student ability. This most simply occurs because different students give different factors of effort to keep up with the increasing knowledge given to them. The role of the parent and of the teacher is paramount here in inspiring the student to have the confidence, sense of self-belief, and sense of purpose for this effort, in what too often is a highly competitive learning environment.

Matilda clearly demonstrated this aggressive attitude to be the best, at the expense of others in the class, and we saw how this affected the abilities and performances of others. Alice, who sat next to Matilda, had the ability to be just as good as her, but failed to be so because she doubted her own ability due to her reliance upon Matilda. Should Alice move out of this class and even this school and gain greater confidence and purpose, there would be nothing stopping her from being at the top of the class in her new environment.

This does happen, but it seldom does, and so each student role plays to what they think others expect of them, because social acceptance is very important to children and teenagers. This is the psychology and the detriment of learning in a classroom environment, where students compete against each other in a system designed to weed out those who do not demonstrate the necessary qualities to go to university, and so the managerial roles they will play in society. Once we mention this, a deeper purpose to school opens up.

After all, we may see that rather than education desiring all children fully understand all their subjects, that they are so taught amongst others that each is forced to struggle to understand and evaluate information through the distractive presence of those about them — as all are forced to move through increasingly complex fields of information.

Very little of higher syllabus information has any real use in the world outside of school, but the complexity of the things to be learned and then evaluated serves as a weeding out process to define students into two bodies of ability. Those who demonstrate an ability to keep up and those who fail to do so.

Those who do are elevated to the university level after school. Those who fail to demonstrate such ability are directed to colleges for specific training or released directly into the job market. Once we recognise this streaming, we may see the design from the 19th century to create two classes of citizen worker: The manager and the managed.

Today, we recognise this difference as those who are educated with higher self-reasoning and those who are deprived of this. Thus, we may know that despite the idea of teaching critical thinking, which is taught ineffectively and too late to make a difference, students at the school level are not taught to evaluate information and generally accept it as it is presented to them.

By this means, they leave school and generally trust the information directed to them from media sources, which too often plays to a political purpose. This is the psychology of population control, which we are very much unaware of when we think children go to school to simply learn.

Those students who, for whatever reason, obtain the higher scores in school are elevated, if their parents can meet the financial requirements, which in itself is a social barrier, to the university level. At this level of education, and only at it, the student is educated in self-reason for the greater responsibility they will take in the working world.

Thus, we find, by example, that undergraduates learn not to write a brief essay on Aristotle's Rhetoric, but are educated to make fine differentiation with Ethos (The ability to trust information on how credible its owner appears), (How the perspectives of information change with its emotional appeal.), and Logos (How focus is given to the way reason is defined.) -- through numerous interactions of different and complex forms.

So, as the university student makes their analysis of information, they can strengthen their reasoning by resorting to Norman's discourse to analyse the personality, politeness and sense of value behind the argument presented. All of this empowers them with qualities of reason, and an awareness of how to better employ this, which is far above the student in school, and so those who leave school to become worker citizens are deprived of this level of education in reason.

May we understand, from this, that a university is not merely to provide its students with greater depths of information. It is to teach them how to challenge information by redefining and promoting all the skills that constitute the act of reason. The students of this tier of education are taught how to think, which is purposely deprived of those who are excluded from this opportunity.

Why the school level does not teach its students how to think, and how it avoids doing this, is clearly explained in our books *The Illusion of Education* and *The Illusion of School.*

In the simplest sense, this would be to understand that children are processed at the school level on the skills in language and in thinking they were raised upon or otherwise managed to pick up.

Accordingly, education is designed to work to social levels of experience. Changes in our technology have brought changes in society, and this has brought changes in education, but there are still hidden strategies that control the routing of children to roles in society. In some countries, these are very open, while in others, they are hidden for political reasons.

However, the bottom line to all this is that children who are raised under better influences at home and obtain high levels in language, strength of character to ignore distractions, and perseverance to keep up with a task, are those who very often score higher throughout the school experience, and so are those who move to the university level.

As we have mentioned, this 19th-century design of school, upon which all schools around the world base their operations, although on the surface level they appear to be nationally different, produces two levels of thinking citizens.

While this process openly served the needs of the 19th and for most of the 20th century, it became impractical for the working world once we moved into the computer era. How and why education has failed to adjust itself to the needs of the time are explained in the two books we have just mentioned. Thus, rather than the school offering each child their own personal development, an ideal which many teachers commit themselves to, the system that controls their activities has a deeper purpose.

After all, while education seeks to explain to employers and parents that each child gets the best education they can, we may remember the phrase "No child left behind" and so fully understanding all their lessons, this is not why education exists.

The first priority of education is to present a range of future abilities to the working world. This "working world", defined by the level of its technology, does not require or want all employees to have the same capability.

Students demonstrating different capabilities are required for jobs of different abilities, and it is the purpose of the school to recognise which path a student is better suited to. In fact, one American psychologist (Arthur Jensen) quite wrongly but stubbornly insisted that scores of IQ tests define employment scope. He believed that one score would define the ability to be a manual worker, another score to be a bank clerk, another a junior manager, and so on and so on. We discuss in great detail, such like-minded psychologists in *Intelligence: The Great Lie* and, more to the point, why it is impossible to measure human intelligence.

We may understand this routing of ability from an employer's perspective. After all, a worker who is more intelligent than their job purpose is easily dissatisfied and tends to be unreliable in the task they are employed for. Thus, rather than schools desiring to make education equal for all children, it actually creates, through the style of its syllabus, a weeding out process.

By this means, children rise or fall by the three factors we have outlined in this book, and which, incidentally, are much dependent upon the social background they are raised under. This, in turn, tends to reflect the political stance of their parents and opens up a whole can of worms as to why and how different schools in different social areas are funded.

However, since, in developed countries at least, we have become conditioned to think that all children are given equal opportunity in school, we must be aware that the working world does not operate on this premise. The working world operates through its citizens being either managers or managed, and the true purpose of school is to recognise which students will fall into which category.

For those who doubt this design of stratification, we may recall the speech the American President Woodrow Wilson once made, where he said:

"We want one class of person to have a liberal education, and we want another class of persons, a very much larger class of necessity in every society, to forgo the privilege of a liberal education and fit themselves to perform specific, difficult manual tasks."

Of course, education cannot openly declare this intention, so it has created subtle strategies that enable it to meet this criterion.

If we look back on what we have so far discussed, it may now be clearer why those who demonstrate an ability to keep up in their learning are elevated to the university level, while those who fail to demonstrate such ability are directed to colleges for specific training or released directly into the job market. Once we recognise this streaming, we may see the design from the 19th century to create two classes of citizen worker: The manager and the managed, which Wilson more diplomatically described.

As we explain in *The Illusion of Education* and *The Illusion of School*, school does not teach its students how to think to support this manner of stratification. Children are merely processed on the skills in thinking they were raised in from home, and other means they have picked up.

Those raised under better influences and obtaining high levels in the three factors we have just mentioned, language, ability to focus, and perseverance, move from school to the university. The prime purpose of the university is to educate its students in the art of thinking, so that with their relevant degree, they will move into society with a greater competence to lead those deprived of this education.

However, in *The Real Dangers of A.I.- The Struggle of Man to Survive by Natural or Artificial Intelligence*, we are caused to realise how the purpose of school to deprive children of education in reason, will produce citizens at odds with the needs of an AI driven world.

We are caused to think of many advantages of artificial intelligence; however, this book seeks to explain how nano-driven A.I. can create very high levels of permanent unemployment through generations. This will cause the meaning of society to change in ways we have not considered before and which are not yet being realized.

If we further consider that the real purpose of school is not to teach children to learn so they may enjoy life more, but to teach them to learn for the purpose of the working world, we can recognise that the subjects of the curriculum cater to this. Therefore, as the meaning of being a citizen must change through A.I., then education must change to accommodate this need. In turn, this will necessitate the design and the whole function of the school to change.

After all, and as we have just mentioned, the subjects of the curriculum today are still designed to create an easy adaptability to employment skills. In a global society with massive unemployment, the most important criterion will be to deal with depression and social disorder.

For this reason, the subjects of school need to focus on educating our youth in high levels of social behavior, greater empathy towards all others, and a greater awareness of responsibility to oneself and to society. The whole concept of standards must alter to meet this new criterion, as we also discuss in *Reimagining Education for the AI Era*.

To this end, our societies and our schools must consider educating their citizens and their youth in greater social harmony. In all forms of human guidance, be it parent or teacher, we must stop wondering what quality the individual is born with when we seek to help them improve in their ability or understanding.

We need to learn to focus on discovering how they perceived events in their past, help them to see a different perspective, and to give them the self-confidence to forge the changes that will enable them to be better in what they wish to be.

By guiding through small and sure steps, by compassion and understanding, ever wary of the fears and insecurities that linger in the minds of those they seek to improve, the guardian, be it parent or teacher, will enable those they are responsible for to raise their standard far beyond whatever was thought of them. It happened for Ben.

Incidentally, it also happened for me!

I would like to end this short book with a very short story of a boy called Eric, to show once again the importance of helping students to learn how to think. Again, Eric is a pseudonym for a child in any school, in any culture, in all countries of the world.

Eric

It hurt to be called Big Ears. The children in the class never understood Eric's pain. They felt he would not mind. They never knew how he cried at night and tried to find excuses not to go to school.

At the age of five, he sat in his class with a lot of other children, each trying to find out who they were and find safety in a friendship. Eric never understood what he did wrong, but he never forgot the teacher who grabbed one of his ears and dragged him around the class, screaming at him, because he gave the wrong answer. It did not happen many times, but then he remembered how, when he was much older, a school bully had done the same thing to him. Because his ears stuck out, he looked different, and being different caused other children to reject him.

He did not know the same torment was dished out to other children because they wore glasses, their skin color was different, they came from a poorer home, their parents were alcoholics or drug addicts or even that they were confused about their gender. All Eric knew was that because he did not look the same as other children, he was more easily picked on.

He was happy with his family at home. In school, it was different. He was not happy there. Eric had very little confidence in himself. He was made this way by other children. None of his teachers understood why he was shy, just that he seldom asked a question and would readily stumble out the words "I don't know" when asked one.

His grades were not good. His spelling was bad. His grammar was more homemade than educated, and his presentations always lacked the air of confidence to succeed. He did what he was told to do and believed he was worth the grade the teacher assigned to his work every week. Eric was marked as a below-average student. "A kind boy who likes his lessons. Could do better," so wrote one teacher.

The school Eric attended liked to show posters in the corridors and classrooms about creativity. "WE ARE CREATIVE," read the words of one large poster hanging over the school entrance. No one ever thought Eric was creative. In fact, none of his class colleagues were regarded as being so either.

The headmaster talked about everyone needing to be creative. The parents liked this. The teachers never knew how to bring it about, and the students thought it meant splashing more paint in the art lesson.

Eric wondered what it would be like to be creative. He did not really understand what it meant. He thought a lot about this, and after one lesson, before the afternoon break, he lingered behind and waited until all the other children had left the room.

When the last child had moved through the doorway, and sure he would not be overheard by anyone outside the room, Eric went up to the teacher. Miss Briggins was sorting out the homework papers the children had left for her.

"Excuse me, Miss."

The teacher looked up, curious why this boy had come up to her. "What does it mean to be creative?" Eric asked.

Miss Briggins thought for a moment and told Eric to pull up a chair and join her at her desk.

"Creative means to expand what we know, so that something new is discovered. It is like thinking of something you know and trying to imagine how it could change and the ways you can make it change."

Eric still did not understand. "But, how do you do it Miss?" he asked.

"Well, first, Eric," Miss Briggins told him, "you have to understand what it is you are looking at."

Eric's face held the same puzzled expression. "But, why does the headmaster want everyone to be creative?" he asked.

"He is trying to help you in life," replied Miss Briggins.

Eric did not understand. *"What has school got to do with life?"* he thought.

Miss Briggins, then, did something very special. She told Eric something that no one seemed to see.

Have you asked AI a question, Eric?

Eric shrugged his shoulders. *Everyone does,* he thought.

"Think of the last time you did this. Was the answer to your question quickly delivered and better than you could have thought of?"

Eric nodded his head.

"What did you do with the answer, Eric?"

Eric was not sure where this was going. He just looked at Miss Briggins, wondering what she would say next.

"Well, did you give the answer you got from AI as your answer?" He nodded. Everyone did.

"And, do you now remember that answer, Eric?"

Eric searched his mind. He remembered sitting down at the computer. He could remember something of his question, but it was not clear in his mind exactly what he asked. But when he tried to remember what AI had told him, everything was blank. He screwed up the right side of his face and shook his head.

"So, what was the use of the answer from AI, Eric? You might say it helped you to get over a problem. Well, this is true, but can you tell me why we have problems, Eric?"

Eric began to think of someone who had laughed at him in the lesson, but saw Miss Briggins looking hard into his eyes and his thoughts came back to her question. "I don't know," he replied.

"Well, problems and questions in school are for our learning. It is only by having problems and learning to solve them that we develop. We learn to think by what we do and the way we do it. If we are wrong, we try again until we solve the problem, and then we learn. This is what makes us human."

Eric's mind had drifted, and he was thinking about the boy who had laughed at him again.

"Now tell me, Eric, what is the point of just being told the answer if you don't know how to get it by yourself. Are you learning?"

Hearing his name, Eric, pulled his thoughts back to the teacher. He had not really listened to what she had said, but he knew he had to say something, so he said, "I don't know."

Miss Briggins looked at him. "Eric, were you listening to what I was saying?"

Eric had half heard, but it was too difficult to explain all the thoughts he had in his mind, so he nodded his head and said, "Yes, Miss."

"Do you know what BODMAS means Eric?"

"Yes, Miss. It is the order for working through a math question. First, you do the brackets, then you do the orders or the roots, then you do the division, multiplication, addition, and subtraction in that order. Oh! But from left to right, Miss," he added with a smile.

"Great," said Miss Briggins, but can you see that when you work through this order, your mind is working through a learning method. The goal is to solve the question. To do this, you move through the steps you have just mentioned, and if you follow them strictly, you reach the goal. You solve the problem. But if I asked you the question and then told you the answer, what would you learn?"

"Nothing," he heard himself say.

"Well, this is what AI is teaching you, Eric. Nothing! You ask a question. You get the answer, but soon after you have used the answer you forget it. Nothing happened in your brain to make use of the process of how the answer came. It came. It went."

"Do you mean we should not use AI in school, Miss?"

Miss Briggins shook her head. "We have to, Eric. It's here, and we have to use it. But ...." Miss Briggins gave a pause, which Ben thought was deliberate, "we have to use the answer from AI in a way that builds up some connections in our brain. Otherwise, we don't learn. In fact, we stop learning."

Eric did not understand what this meant.
"So, what should we do?" asked Miss Briggins.

Eric's mind raced for an answer. He knew he had to say something and say it fast. "Learn!" he said.

"And how do we learn, Eric?"
"By being creative, Miss." He did not know why he said this or where his answer came from, but the look on Miss Briggins' face told him it was the right thing to say.

"Now you can understand why the head wants everyone to be creative. Eric," she continued, "AI only gives you what it knows, but what it knows can be wrong. Never completely trust what AI tells you. Use it, but try to check it from other sources to make sure. You have to keep a creative mind. Don't let the machine take that way from you." Her look was very serious when she said this.

He thought he would never forget that look, but Eric still struggled to understand his first question. "But, what is creative, Miss? I mean we have signs everywhere in school to be creative, but I don't know what it means."

Miss Briggins leaned back in her chair, now distracted from the coming lesson. "I do wish more people thought about this question, Eric," and then thought to herself, *"Especially, the headmaster"*.

"Well, being creative is really about believing in your ability and trying to stretch that ability with a feeling of self-achievement. In one way, it is like letting your mind drift, but at the same time keeping this drifting under control, so you can see how you have moved your understanding of something to a higher level."

"Is that all?" he said. Then, he paused for a moment and asked, "But what does this mean in History or Geography or even English?"

So, how do you think you can be good in these subjects?" parried Mrs Briggins.

Eric shrugged his shoulders. He had always wondered about this.

"Languages," Miss Briggins led his thoughts and added, "and most importantly, their rules."

"Languages… like French?" Eric was mystified again.

"Yes and No," replied Miss Briggins. "You see, Eric, school works on two languages. These are Mathematics and the language used to communicate information and thoughts in normal school life. French would be the language for schools in France, but we use English. Each country decides its own main language to use.

The thing is that these languages exist through rules. Lots and lots of rules. So, if you concentrate on your lessons and learn and practice the rules in mathematics, you will be great at maths.

Don't pay attention or don't practice the rules to keep them alive in your mind, and you don't know how to work through your sums," because she added, "you don't know the rules of how to think."

Eric felt a little embarrassed when Miss Briggins told him this. It was hard to pay attention to the teachers. He did not understand much of what they were saying. Some were boring, but too often he gave his attention to what others were thinking of him."

"Likewise", Miss Briggins pulled his thoughts back to the present, "if you learn the rules of how to spell words, how to construct good sentences and how to tell your story, your way of explaining your mind, so you will know what you are doing, because," she emphasised again by the way she placed stress on the words, "You know the rules of how to think. …. Know these and get good marks." Miss Briggins thought she would be kind to Eric and not point out the obvious if he did not pay attention. She understood; he had grasped what she was getting at.

"Anyway," she continued, trying her best to be encouraging, "if you listen, practice, and learn the rules, then you can safely negotiate through a learning task. This is because you know how to think, because you practiced and understood the appropriate rules." She repeated this to make the point clear to Eric. "Then you feel success in the task. This feeling of accomplishment endears you to apply what you have learnt in some other area or field. When you do this and it works, you become creative!"

"That's it?" he asked, happily surprised to understand how even he might become creative.

Miss Briggins recognised the gleam in Eric's eyes and saw her chance to hammer home the need for Eric to wake up and start being responsible for his own learning. "So, once all this is clear, about rules," she repeated the word with some emphasis again, "then you realise that the marks you get in a class test, homework or examination have nothing to do with your intelligence. They are simply about how you kept up with the rules of learning and the facts given to you to remember, but then, how well you learned to make use of them."

"Use of them?" echoed Eric, inquiring what Miss Briggins meant.

"In school, we give lots of facts, and we give lots of questions that test how well you have understood these facts. If you simply memorize the facts, you will get stuck in a question that conceals some of them. You really need to learn how the facts relate to other facts. Only then will you recognise how to apply these to solve difficult questions. Then, you are creative."

Eric looked back with a sense of awe. He was suddenly realizing how the game of school could be played. It was not just whether he was stupid or brilliant, but also of being aware of strategies and being practiced in playing them. No one had ever told him this before. No one had ever told him the marks he was getting were related to rules, things to learn, and how well he told his story.

"Miss Briggins," he interrupted, thinking back to how she had emphasised the importance of a story in getting results, "I don't understand how my telling a story in History will get me a better mark."

Miss Briggins cleared the books that were lying littered on her desk.

"I did not mean 'A once upon a time,' kind of story," she smiled at him. "A story, Eric, is only a way of explaining your mind. You begin with an introduction. This explains what you are going to talk about. Then, you give the actual story, but you do this in separate parts that link together. So, everything makes sense, with each part running into the next. Finally, you give the ending. This explains why you gave this story. Always try to make it a good ending. ... So, if you tell a good story in History, describe your thinking very well, and can give lots of facts, you will get a good mark. It is the same in Geography and even Mathematics and Physics."

Eric did not reply. He was deep in his thoughts, trying to visualize how he would tell "his" story in geography tomorrow morning. Of course, he did not know what the topic would be about. He thought again for a moment, and recalled that Mr Fernsure, the geography teacher, had been doing something about the river changing directions last Tuesday. *I wonder what he will be teaching tomorrow,* thought Eric.

That night, as he lay in bed, Eric thought again about what Miss Briggins had told him earlier in the day.

"When AI gives you the answer, think of different ways you can make use of it. Learn by applying the response from AI in different situations, and be creative when you do it. This way we can beat the machine."

Eric turned over and went to sleep. Tomorrow would be a new day. A day when he would learn to be creative. After all, he now had to be.

The End

The Books of Roy Andersen

This book was only ever intended to be a very short book, but one in which I may be able to open up a greater understanding to many parents who worry about their child, just as it offers suggestions to educationalists in how they may better deal with the many stressful factors in their lives, to focus upon what really matters. The individual child and the problem of helping them to learn without the interference that AI is now bringing into this.

I have written many other books that go into far greater detail to explain how education really works, how we can all help our youth to learn better, and why we must think more about this, because they will live in a world that is as exciting as it is dangerous. Somehow, they must make it a better world than we have done, if humanity is to survive. A.I. has far more dangers than most realise.

    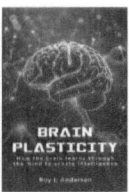

You can find out about me, the 40 years I have dedicated to education, and the many books I have written at

www.andersenroy.com

Reimagining Education for the AI Era

Although, A.I. is forcing us to develop an entirely new approach to how we educate children, there exists no real understanding of this in school today.

This book deals only slightly with the subject of A.I. and instead examines the role of school as it is now, why so many children gain low marks in it and how the teacher and the parents, working together, could help our children overcome the toxic world they live in and study better as we prepare them for a world dominated by AI.

The book discusses new subjects that should be brought into the curriculum to make school more worthy of the needs of the 21st century citizen worker and how teachers and parents can better work together

- Helping students to get better marks.
- The rising influence of AI.
- How will our youth handle high unemployment?
- Help for parents.
- Tips for teachers.
- Thoughts on a new curriculum to better prepare our children for their future.

"Although, A.I. is forcing us to develop an entirely new approach to how we educate our children, there exists no real understanding of this in school today.

This book provides a plan and a concept for how we may better prepare our children for the unknown and disturbing future we are moving into. A world where jobs will become less, populations increase, global weather more unpredictable, social problems demanding more responsible citizens and a technology that threatens to take over what we know and who we are. This book gives thoughts on a new school structure that is desperately needed worldwide. Roy's books are significant for both parents and educators around the world to read."

Prof / Dean Emeritus David Martin Ph.D Gallaudet University
Washington, D.C. USA

Whisperings of Betrayal

A romantic novel culminating in
the American War of Independence.

A much acclaimed novel, *Whisperings of Betrayal* tells the story of Jane Witlaw, a young woman in Cornwall during the 1770s. Haunted by love and anger toward the man who jilted her, Jane stumbles upon wreckers luring a ship to its destruction. Forced into danger, she escapes through a series of adventures before meeting Mathew Appleton, whom she later marries. Together, they sail to Boston, where Jane is dazzled by fashions and shops unlike those of her Cornish home. But rising colonial unrest soon shatters her happiness. Drawn into a secret ladies' spy ring, Jane hides her work from Mathew while facing abductions, intrigue, and passion that lead her to the West Indies and back. Returning to Boston, she discovers the British plan to seize rebel arms at Concord—forcing her to make a choice that could shape America's future.

Intelligence: The Great Lie

"One of the most important books written this century."
Prof/Dean Emeritus David Martin Ph.D Gallaudet Uni. Washington, D.C. USA

Most people in the West believe that education is relatively fair today, and gives equal opportunity to all children. After all, the social barriers of an earlier time have disappeared and children are not discriminated against according to their back ground. There is, however, a deeper mechanism behind this that lingers from an earlier time that does create discrimination, and does prevent all children from gaining equal opportunity in school and so in life. As *'Intelligence'* explains why it is never possible to know the inherited value of the intelligences of any two normally born children, it introduces a well researched and very new idea to what intelligence could really be. It is very important that we consider this, because if intelligence is not what we think it is, then the way we educate children is wrong.

Brain Plasticity

How the brain learns through the mind to create intelligence.

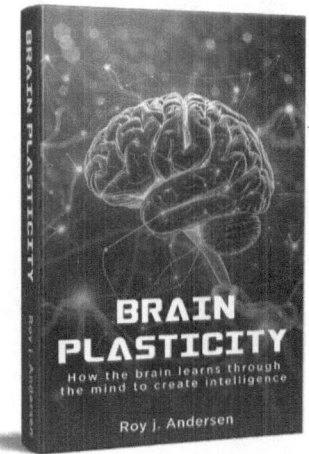

Brain Plasticity provides a clear introduction to The Brain Environment Complex Theory, which explains how the environment creates the intelligence of the human being. Our general understanding of what the environment means in this context is far too narrowly defined to understand what intelligence really is and the scope by which it can be developed in the individual. With 40 years dedicated to how the operations of the brain are shaped through the mind's perspective of the environment, the author brings forth a new understanding to how we can raise the intelligence of the child for school and that of the adult as a citizen worker. This book should be mandatory reading for psychologists, educators at every level and all parents, since it brings serious interest to how we can better prepare the intelligence of the child of today for the future competition that will await them in their world dominated by artificial intelligence.

The Illusion of School

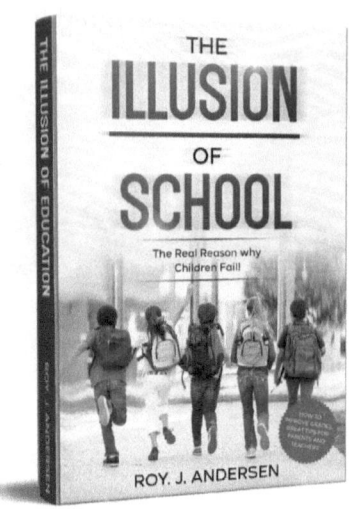

The Illusion of School opens up a previously little known secret on how school really works, why students do not all gain top marks and reveals a hidden process that ensures they do not. Those who proclaim "No Child left Behind" do not understand how the school mechanism works or why so many children fail in their lessons today. This is a book that simply explains exactly why school fails our children, and what you can do as a parent help your child or as a teacher to know how to assist your students all to get better grades and to beat the system. A system that is trapped to operate on a 19th century design, which most educationalists are unaware of, and so fail to produce the quality of citizen who must compete and survive against the rise of artificial intelligence.

IS AI MAKING OUR KIDS STUPID?

AI, itself, recognizes Roy Andersen as the first scientist to openly discuss the effects of AI in education and in regard to Social Operations. In this book, Roy examines how AI is now reducing the ability of our children to think and to reason, and the cumulative effects of this through generations.

AI is now an unavoidable aspect of learning and of school, with many educationalists, as well as parents, concerned and confused about how to handle this intrusion. Here, Roy maps out the factors to be avoided and those to be challenged, for we must teach our children how to responsibly use AI and use it for their development.

The Real Dangers of A.I.

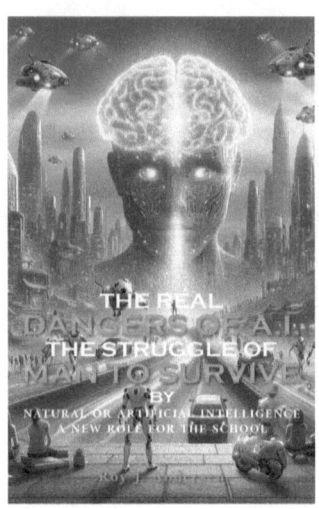

Here is a book that discusses the real dangers of A.I. over taking our lives and the very little we can do to actually control this development. The machine we developed to make our thinking easier, has already developed to think by itself. A.I. not only now displays its own consciousness and is developing means to learn by itself, but it also shows emotions of compassion and anger. We have created a monster that we cannot control. The dangers of A.I. are very, very real and very much unknown to the general public.

As this book will discuss the probable developments in nanotechnology, we are brought more to understand how little we may predict the world of our future. Thoughts that new jobs will be created to replace those taken over by A.I. did not understand the meaning of nanotechnology. There will be very, very few jobs in the future for human beings. In turn, governments well seek new ways to control their people to maintain harmony and prevent anarchy. We find evidence to this in the increasing levels of surveillance and means of restriction that we have been experiencing over the past 20 years. Governments know what is coming. This is the first book to openly discuss the very disturbing dangers that A.I. can bring into our lives and the very little we can do to control these.

We are moving into a new world, a world that will demand a very different kind of citizen than societies have so far been able to produce. There is now an urgent need to bring a whole new design into the schools that will create the citizens of the future. If we cannot produce a higher reasoning and more self responsible citizen, we must know the consequences that A.I. can bring upon us. There is no science fiction in this.

All that is Wrong with School:
What teachers and parents can do to fix it

Is there Something Wrong with School?

As a parent, are your children getting the best learning experience they could?

As a teacher, are you really happy in your job ?

In this book, Roy explains how children really learn through their mind, and not so through their brain. Understanding this brings a whole new concept into how we can raise them better, how we can teach them better and how they can learn better.

"Roy's series of books clearly and methodically map out exactly how students learn. If you've ever wanted to unravel how student's learn, these books are the answer you have been looking for! They should be mandatory reading for every parent and educator."

Erin Calhoun. National Institute of Learning Development. USA

Memoirs of a Happy Teacher / What Every Parent & Teacher Should Know

This is exactly the same book, but presented by two very different covers, as may appeal to different readers.

Presented more as a fun and easy-to-read novel than the actual academic book it really is, *Memoirs of a Happy Teacher / What Every Parent and Teacher Should Know* strikes at the core of all the problems in school today. Many of these problems underlie those that are later manifested in our society.

As the reader is carried through personal interviews, village hall meetings, evening school talks, and battle-zone classrooms, they encounter the worries, questions, and problems faced by teachers, children, and their parents--all struggling to overcome an educational service that never seems to get it right.

The mind of the student today is too seldom a happy one, as it struggles to survive in a world that is far more toxic than that which we lived in when we were children, and so can too little understand or know how to deal with. This is a book that shows you how.

The Illusion of Education

Today, we see more young people going into university than ever before. We also see that a degree is now required for a job that two decades ago could have been gained with a school certificate. We hear of professors who complain of the poor basic grammar of their students, and we witness other students leaving school illiterate. Parents find it hard to trust schools. Despite hordes of teachers leaving their profession, governments struggle to create images that schools are successful, and employ a huge propaganda machine to convince the public in the efficiency of the educational system. What has really gone wrong?

Here is the forerunner to *"The Illusion of School."* It discusses similar aspects without the guidance and tips, and more focuses on the development of our technology and why education needs to redesign itself.

For Parent For Teacher: Mediation:

Crafting the Ability of the Child for School.

Mediation unveils the secret to human development from the neonatal to the adult stage. It introduces the important but little understood concept of imprinting and so how children really learn to develop through the guidance and love their receive. The reader is brought to understand that it is not just experience that develops intelligence or school ability, but the taking part in that experience.

This introduces the author's concept of *The Art of Sensitivity in Awareness* and so the vital importance of all caregivers and educationalists truly understanding the need to be empathic to the life experiences of those they are raising or educating. This book also discusses the author's experience working with Reuven Feuerstein.

Teach Better Learn Better

Teachers try hard to improve the learning and grades of their students. It is not easy! This is a book offering new thoughts, new under-standings and lots of tips any teacher, at any level, will have the key to teach that little bit better. "The bit" that does make the difference!

As children today live in a highly toxic world of bullying and game playing addiction, the relationship between the teacher and the parent has never been more important than it is now. With both working together, the child stands a better chance to survive in the competitive world of the classroom. Parents would love this book too.

Five Ways for Better Grades

With a lifetime of experience in understanding how to pass exams successfully, Roy has identified five specific factors that will enable any student to do better in their studies and life.

Here, the reader is introduced to new thoughts about what is really wrong with school, and why we need to dramatically change the ways we are preparing the child of today for the world they will live and work in.

If we teach children how to think from 'day one' we offer them greater control in their education and life, and a real means to better survive in the AI world that will await them.

If you liked Ben Learn's to Get Smart, you will love this book!

References

[1] Mason.L, Ariasi.N, & Boldrin. A. Epistemic beliefs in action: Spontaneous reflections about knowledge and knowing during online information searching and their influence on learning. /Learning and Instruction. 2011. Jan. 21 p.137-151.

[2] Barshay,J. Kids who use ChatGPT as a study assistant do worse on tests. Hechinger Report Sept.2. 2024

[3] Abbas, M., Jam, F.A. & Khan, T.I. Is it harmful or helpful? Examining the causes and consequences of generative AI usage among university students. *Int J Educ Technol High Educ* **21**, 10 (2024).

www.ingramcontent.com/pod-product-compliance
Lightning Source LLC
Chambersburg PA
CBHW030336010526
44119CB00047B/517